dreams &
DESTINY

–A Study in Daniel

John L. Benson

ACCENT ON LIFE
BIBLE CURRICULUM

ADULT STUDENT
Bible Study Guide

This Bible Study Guide is a part of a ten-year adult curriculum designed to assist you in making the entire Bible your Guide for daily living.

John L. Benson/Author
James T. Dyet/Executive Editor
Robert L. Mosier/Publisher

Accent on Life Bible Curriculum
Accent-B/P Publications
12100 W. Sixth Avenue
P.O. Box 15337
Denver, Colorado 80215

ISBN 0-89636-014-8

CONTENTS

The Destiny of Faithful Men

1

LESSON SCRIPTURE
Daniel 1

RELATED SCRIPTURE
II Chronicles 36; Isaiah 39:5-7; Jeremiah
25:1-14; 52; Hebrews 11

LESSON AIM
To refuse to compromise our convictions.

LEARN BY HEART
"But Daniel purposed in his heart that he
would not defile himself with the portion of
the king's meat, nor with the wine which
he drank" (Daniel 1:8).

STUDENT'S NOTEBOOK

This column is for the
student who desires
additional study of
the lesson theme.

EVERY DAY WITH THE WORD

Monday	The depths of sin	Ezekiel 8
Tuesday	The result of sin	Jeremiah 25:1-14
Wednesday	The cure for sin	Romans 5
Thursday	The way of faithfulness	I Peter 1:13-25
Friday	The power for faithfulness	Romans 8
Saturday	The example of faithfulness	Hebrews 11
Sunday	The result of faithfulness	James 2:14-26

LESSON PREPARATION

Have you ever been in a place where nobody
knew you and thought, "Good, now I don't have

to be so careful about what I do''? Perhaps it was your first year at college, or when you moved into a new city, or on that vacation trip last year. Maybe you were thinking that, at least for a little while, your responsibility to be faithful to God was not as great as it used to be. This inconsistency in the life of many believers has caused one man to define a Christian as ''one who follows the teachings of Christ in so far as they are not inconsistent with a life of sin.'' Is this the kind of witness we give to those who watch our life?

Daniel illustrates the results of a life that was consistent in its witness to God. Through all his temptations he remained faithful, and he was rewarded.

A man's character is determined by what he does when no one is watching. His reputation is determined by what others actually see.

DANIEL'S ADVENTURES
(Daniel 1:1-7)

Although Daniel was in right relationship with God, this was not true of the nation as a whole. Their sin had become so great that God had carried out the judgment which He had predicted many years before (Isaiah 39:6,7). Daniel, through no fault of his own, found himself a captive in a foreign land and exposed to many practices that were contrary to the Word of God. Because of his family position and his physical and mental ability, he was chosen for training by the Babylonians (Daniel 1:4).

From the beginning of Israel's history, God had promised judgment if the nation would not obey the law (Deuteronomy 28:15-62; 31:16-21).

This training involved instruction in a very complicated language and learning what was considered the greatest wisdom of the day. The Chaldeans were considered specialists in the fields of magic and astrology. If Daniel became successful

Daniel belonged to the tribe from which Messiah would come—the royal line of Judah (verse 6).

in this, it meant that although he was still a captive, his life would be rather easy and that he would occupy a preferred place in Babylon.

The problem that faced Daniel was that the training involved eating what was contrary to the Mosaic law (verse 5). The delicacy of the food was not the issue, for it was the same that the king himself ate. Something about it, however, would have caused Daniel to defile himself if he had eaten it. Daniel now had a choice to make: should he do what he knew was wrong, or should he jeopardize his whole future by remaining true to God and requesting some other kind of food? The other Jewish youths were eating the food without complaint or conscience (verse 10). Could he afford to be any different? After all, his captors might return him to the resettlement camps for his defiance and inappreciation.

DANIEL'S ABSTINENCE
(Daniel 1:8-21)

Daniel did not delay his decision. He determined there would be no compromise (Daniel 1:8). This is a reflection of his past way of life. Because he had been faithful in the past, it was easier for him to make the right decision at this point.

He proposed to the one in charge of his training that they have a ten-day trial period (verse 12). During the ten days he would follow his own diet. If at the end he was in poorer condition than the other captives, he would then eat the king's food. This involved some danger to those responsible

The number 10 seems to be associated with trial and testing. See Revelation 2:10 and consider the ten plagues in Egypt.

for Daniel. If something happened to him and the king found out about it, it would cost them their lives (verse 10). But God caused Daniel's request to receive a favorable response on the part of his captors (verse 9). Thus, in spite of the danger to themselves, they allowed Daniel and his three friends to eat only those foods which the four Hebrews chose.

In a day of easy living and willing compromise, Daniel's life stands out. He resolved to be different if this was what remaining true to God required. His goal was not to please men and get a few compliments but to please God and live a life of which God could approve. He guarded against the shortsighted approach to life which sacrifices the eternal on the altar of the present.

Romans 15:1,3; Galatians 1:10; Ephesians 6:6; Colossians 3:22; II Timothy 2:4

Daniel's whole life was above reproach. Not a single sin is recorded against him. We are not to imagine that he was actually sinless, but we are to appreciate that his deepest motive was to glorify God. His eye was single; therefore, his whole body was full of light.

I Corinthians 10:31

In Daniel's refusal to conform he did not approach his supervisor in an arrogant and defiant manner. He made no assault upon the Babylonian religion. He did not assume a sanctimonious superiority. Instead, he requested that he might be permitted to abstain from defiling himself (verse 8). He was gracious and tactful, yet firm and uncompromising. He was careful not to do anything that would get his supervisor into trouble with the king at the risk of losing his life. This is a lesson we all need to learn. God does not expect us to antagonize the enemies of the gospel by our rash and belligerent attitudes.

What principles do you see in Daniel's approach which will guide you in your witnessing and in your relationships with your unsaved employer? See Ephesians 6:5 and I Peter 2:18.

Daniel and his friends did not protest the

change of their names to correspond with heathen deities. The Babylonian idolators could call them what they liked; names could never hurt them, but to displease God by eating food which had probably been offered to demons was an act which they could not contemplate.

And what was the outcome? God in His providence directly intervened in several matters. First, He prepared the heart of Melzar to grant Daniel's request. This proves that God has access to the minds and wills of even unregenerate men and can control them as He wills. What Melzar chose to do of his own free will was exactly what God had chosen for him to do.

Second, God sustained Daniel and his brethren so that they suffered no ill effects from such a poor diet. Expecting them to show signs of malnutrition, Melzar found the quartet of captives in better health than those who had gorged themselves on the king's delicacies. In all of the rest of their training they were not required to share the king's diet. They continued to live on their simple fare, and God continued to preserve their bodily well-being.

Third, God gave Daniel and his friends all sorts of knowledge and skills. They surpassed everyone else in the kingdom in their knowledge of the Chaldean language, literature, art, crafts, and sciences. Archaeology has demonstrated that ancient Babylon had made tremendous strides in grammar, mathematics, astronomy, and the sciences. In these the young men were thoroughly instructed. But even though they had a three-year course in liberal arts which gave them proficiency in all the humanities, they never adopted the philosophy or the religion of the Chaldeans. God

Warning: Don't imagine that God will sustain us when we foolishly or willfully abuse our health by a poor diet.

Moses was instructed in all the learning of Egypt. In the providence of God this was necessary for the purpose Moses was to fulfill. Likewise, God's appointed place for Daniel required this kind of preparation. What other Biblical characters were educated men?

gave them a penetrating insight into the nature of reality, and they enjoyed from Him discriminative powers which natural men lacked.

Fourth, God gave an additional ability to Daniel. He was made to understand all visions and dreams (verse 17). This endowment was a prerequisite to what follows in the book of Daniel.

Fifth, God providentially arranged the elevation of Daniel and his companions to places of prominence in the Babylonian government. Every detail of a long line of events worked toward this end. God was working out His eternal purposes, and the details called for a Jewish prime minister and prophet to counsel several pagan kings and disclose to them (and us) the course of world empires.

Ephesians 1:11

Was there something in Daniel naturally that commended him to God and merited him such distinction? Of course not! Whatever qualifications Daniel had for the task that lay before him, God bestowed upon him in grace. What made Daniel different from the mass of Jewish captives that he should be selected for special service? Was it some meritorious virtue in himself like faithfulness? No! God made the difference between Daniel and those who forsook the Lord. The God of Daniel caused him to be born into a royal family. The God of Daniel caused him to be transported to Babylon with the rest of the men of Judah. God caused the head of the eunuchs to permit Daniel's request. We may safely say that God put it in Daniel's mind to make such a request, and God by His own divine power produced steadfastness and resolve in Daniel not to conform to Babylonian customs. Thank God for Daniel's faithfulness!

Daniel outlived the empire which took him captive.

FOOD FOR THOUGHT

"Whenever you face a decision you have three chances: Do what you please; do what others do; or do what is right."

—A Banningism

NOW TEST YOUR KNOWLEDGE

Match the following:
1. Daniel's immediate supervisor was _____.
2. The priestly administrators were called _____.
3. Nebuchadnezzar had defeated _____.
4. Daniel's new, heathen name was _____.
5. Daniel and his three friends had come from the city of _____.
6. The prince and master of the eunuchs was _____.
7. Daniel chose to eat _____.
8. One special ability Daniel had was interpreting _____.
9. Daniel was favored by the Babylonians because of _____.
10. "Chaldean" is either a language or a _____.

a. Jehoiakim	f. languages	k. Ashpenaz
b. soothsayers	g. intellect	l. God
c. Jerusalem	h. city	m. caste
d. visions	i. Melzar	n. vegetables
e. Chaldeans	j. Belteshazzar	

World Empires in Preview

2

LESSON SCRIPTURE
Daniel 2

RELATED SCRIPTURE
Daniel 7; Revelation 13; 17

LESSON AIM
To believe, trust, and obey God's Word.

LEARN BY HEART
"Blessed be the name of God for ever and ever: for wisdom and might are his. . . . He revealeth the deep and secret things: he knoweth what is in the darkness, and the light dwelleth with him" (Daniel 2:20,22).

EVERY DAY WITH THE WORD

Monday	The originator of the world	Psalm 136:1-9
Tuesday	The problem with man's rule	Job 24:1-10
Wednesday	The universal rule of God	Psalm 93
Thursday	God's view of man's rule	Daniel 7:1-7
Friday	Present and future rulers	Matthew 4:1-11
Saturday	The end of man's rule	Revelation 19:11-21
Sunday	Final triumph of Christ	Psalm 2

STUDENT'S NOTEBOOK

This column is for the student who desires additional study of the lesson theme.

LESSON PREPARATION

Prophecies, dreams, fortune tellers—how many times have you heard of people trying to learn about the future from these means? They read the cards and attend seances in their desperate struggle to alleviate their fears about the future. It seems that to most people the greatest of all fears is fear of the unknown.

The believer is spared this anxiety because he has been united to Christ. He is in a place of safety that gives the promise of a future in the presence of God Himself. In addition to this, God has given us in the Bible an outline of the future history of the world. Although we do not know all the details, He has nevertheless revealed the general broad outline of the course of events to take place among the nations. Daniel 2 contains the ABC of prophecy; later chapters in Daniel supply the details.

I Corinthians 12:13
Galatians 3:28

God has disclosed to believers what the goal of history will be (Ephesians 1:10).

THE MYSTERY OF THE DREAM
(Daniel 2:1-23)

One night King Nebuchadnezzar had a dream which agitated him so much that he woke up and could not get back to sleep. The king did not know the meaning of the dream, and he was afraid it might mean that something unfavorable was going to happen to him. He called his wise men and asked them to interpret his dream. They were willing to interpret provided the king would tell them the content of the dream (Daniel 2:4).

The king had apparently forgotten the dream, and so he used this as an occasion to test the reliability of his wise men. He demanded to know the content of the dream and the meaning of it. If they could tell it to him, their reward would be great. If they could not, then the king would have them all killed (verses 5,6). Nebuchadnezzar

A few interpreters take the view that Nebuchadnezzar knew the content of the dream but refused to divulge it to his wise men.

knew that these men could say almost anything, and he would have no way to check on their interpretation. But if they could produce both the dream and its import, he would be convinced of their ability to know the secrets of the future and to advise him correctly and wisely (verses 7-9).

The wise men replied that the king's request was beyond the power of any human being. In fact, they claimed, only the gods could reveal the dream to the king; and unfortunately, the gods did not dwell among men (verses 10,11). This fired the king's wrath! Now he had proof that his wise men were frauds. He knew that all the information he had received from them in the past was nothing but lies and guesswork. They had been making a fool out of him! Immediately the command went out to kill all the wise men in the city of Babylon (verses 12,13).

Numbered among the wise men were Daniel and his three friends. The man appointed to lead the execution of the king's decree came to Daniel and told him what had happened. Daniel asked to be brought before the king. He then requested that the king give him a little time, and he would reveal the dream and its interpretation (verses 14-16).

Daniel left the presence of the king and held a prayer meeting with his three friends. Their approach to God was based not upon their own merit or their own faithfulness but upon God's mercy. They realized the truth that if we receive anything from God, it is not that we deserve it but that His great mercies are new every morning (verses 17,18).

That night, through a vision, God revealed to Daniel both the dream and its interpretation. Before Daniel rushed off to inform the king or even

The wise men panicked; Daniel and his companions prayed. It seems that Daniel knew the value of united prayer. He also knew the meaning of Psalm 50:15.

his friends of the disclosure, he stopped to praise God, who is the source of all wisdom. What man cannot know God knows (verses 19-23).

THE MEANING OF THE DREAM
(Daniel 2:24-49)

The vision covers a period of time in history known as "The Times of the Gentiles." It began with the captivity of Judah (II Chronicles 36) and ends with the second coming of Christ to the earth. See Luke 21:24.

Daniel went before the king and introduced the interpretation by comparing the limited knowledge of man with the unlimited knowledge of God (Daniel 2:27,28). He wanted Nebuchadnezzar to understand that he was about to receive information concerning the latter days that could not be discovered by human means—it must come through a special revelation from God. Daniel gave all of the credit to God.

Before explaining the meaning of the dream, Daniel gave a resume of its content (verses 31-35). The king had seen an image (a colossus) in the form of a man. Its composition consisted of various kinds of metals: gold, silver, bronze, and iron mixed with clay. While he was looking at the image, Nebuchadnezzar saw a stone strike the feet of the image, crumbling the whole image. The stone then became larger and larger until it filled the entire earth.

The image represents all the world-ruling empires that would come into existence from Daniel's time until the second advent of Christ. This is clearly expressed in verse 28 in the phrase "latter days." The term is used in the Old Testament generally to refer to a future time of trouble and blessing for the nation Israel. Here, in keeping with the context, it refers to the last days of Gentile dominion over the earth.

The metals in the image represent (1) the progressive decentralization of authority in each of the successive governments and (2) the general decrease in strength of the governments. Nebuchadnezzar possessed absolute dictatorial power; his eventual successors, Darius and Cyrus, had to work within the framework of the laws of the Medes and Persians.

We are not left in any doubt about the historic starting point of the period which this dream disclosed. By beginning his interpretation with the head of gold and by associating it with Nebuchadnezzar, Daniel indicates that the Babylonian empire is the first of those kingdoms which will make up the time of the Gentiles (verse 38). Many records have been discovered which confirm the greatness and grandeur of his kingdom. His hanging gardens constituted one of the seven wonders of the ancient world. It is thought that he had them constructed for his wife, who in the arid flatland of Babylon was homesick for the hills of the area in which she was reared. The walls of the city of Babylon were so thick that the top easily accommodated a chariot race. All of the magnificence and wealth of his empire will characterize the final stage of man's rule upon the earth.

The second and third empires are not identified in this chapter (verse 39). We are told later, however, what empires are meant. In Daniel 5:28, the Medo-Persian empire is predicted to follow the Babylonian; and in 8:21, the successor to Medo-Persia is announced to be Greece. Thus the book of Daniel is proved once again to be both historically and prophetically accurate, for it was written long before some of these empires came into existence. The Persian invasion from the East was responsible for conquering Babylon in the past,

Babylon plays an important part, both past and future, in the Bible. Study Isaiah 13; 21:9; 48:14,20; Jeremiah 50:29-46 and Revelation 17—18.

The city occupied an area of about 200 square miles. Get further details from a Bible dictionary.

Compare Isaiah 41:25 and 45:1-3 with Revelation 16:12.

and it appears that an invasion from the East will destroy the Babylon of the future.

The fourth kingdom is nowhere identified in the book of Daniel (Daniel 2:40-43). But since up to this point the empires are identical to those empires which all historians recognize—one following the other from Babylon to Greece—we have good reason for thinking that the fourth empire must be identified with the kingdom which immediately followed Greece—Rome. The descriptions fit Rome, for Rome ruled with an iron fist even though as a Republic with a senate it was the weakest form of government yet to appear.

This fourth empire will be studied more particularly in lesson 7. The New Testament discusses it in Revelation 13:1; 17:12.

Note that this chapter does not speak of five empires. The feet and toes are a development of the legs. The legs probably symbolize the division that split the Roman empire into Western and Eastern sections. The legs, feet, and toes are all parts of the one empire. The vision depicts a time in the future when the territory once occupied by Rome will develop into ten distinct parts of a political unification. This development did not occur at any time during Rome's long existence and has not yet occurred. The prophecy points to a time when Western Europe comes under the control of ten rulers who eventually submit to the dictates of a final tyrant.

This time period is further identified by the fact that the occasion in question will be followed immediately by the inauguration of the kingdom of God (verse 44). That kingdom awaits the coming of Jesus Christ (''the stone'') before it will be introduced to history.

It is only consistent to believe that the mountain filling the earth is the millennial kingdom of the future. It is a violation of all the rules of interpreta-

Most interpreters think that Christ is the stone which will

17

tion to make the parts of the image to represent political governments and literal empires functioning on earth and then to interpret, as some do, the kingdom which Messiah will introduce to be a spiritual rule of God in the heart which began at the first advent and culminated in the gospel age.

The coming of the stone could not refer to the first advent of Christ, as many commentaries declare, because the ten-divisioned Roman empire did not exist at that time, nor was the "destructive" work of the stone accomplished during Christ's earthly ministry. This chapter does not teach a gradual spread of the so-called kingdom of grace in the heart through the preaching of the gospel. What we have here is a sudden intervention in history in which Christ comes to smash the final stage of Gentile world dominion and to set up the empire of Heaven on the earth—the visible, literal, political, social, and historical kingdom of God for which the disciples were taught to pray: "Thy kingdom come."

The phrase, "in the days of these kings" (verse 44), is decisive in any attempt to identify the specific time for the introduction of the kingdom which the God of Heaven will set up. These "kings" did not exist at the first advent, and they did not appear in the time of the apostles. They haven't come on the world scene yet. Therefore, the kingdom of God has not been established yet. The kingdom is always and everywhere future. It is designed to replace earthly empires with a divine government which shall proceed from Jerusalem. The coming kingdom will be political and historical, but it will also be spiritual and eternal. Spiritual principles will regulate the affairs of men in that day, and time will merge into

demolish the final stage of the empires of men. See Psalm 118:22; Isaiah 8:14; 28:16; Zechariah 3:9; Matthew 21:42; 25:31; I Peter 2:8; and Revelation 11:15; 19:11-16.

Believers of the church age will participate in the coming kingdom. We shall have an abundant entrance into it; we shall reign with Christ in it.

eternity at the close of the millennial day. One last word is necessary about the kingdom as the Bible uses the expression. It is not Heaven itself. It is not salvation, the new birth, the church, spiritual principles, or Christ's rule in the believer's heart. The kingdom is the earthly millennial reign.

Nebuchadnezzar's reaction to what Daniel had to say was normal for a worshiper of many gods. He began to worship Daniel as the one through whom the gods work (verse 46). Although he was still a believer in many gods, the king recognized Daniel's God as the greatest of all gods (verse 47).

FOOD FOR THOUGHT

"Because of the character and the invincible purpose of God, there can be no doubt of the ultimate triumph of righteousness."
—George W. Truett

NOW TEST YOUR KNOWLEDGE

Choose the correct answers:
1. God communicated to Old Testament men through (a) dreams; (b) visions; (c) prophets; (d) all of these.
2. The image's golden head represented (a) Rome; (b) the church; (c) Satan; (d) Babylon.
3. The silver part of the image represented (a) Greece; (b) Medo-Persia; (c) Heaven; (d) the disciples.
4. The bronze part of the image represented (a) Rome; (b) England; (c) Greece; (d) North America.
5. The iron legs of the image represented (a) Babylon; (b) Rome; (c) the millennial kingdom; (d) Russia.
6. The stone which smites the image represents (a) Satan; (b) the United States; (c) Christ; (d) China.
7. The great mountain which fills the earth is (a) the church; (b) the millennial kingdom; (c) Greece; (d) none of these.
8. The vision pertains to a period which Daniel calls (a) the latter days; (b) the age of grace; (c) the millennium.
9. A future development of the (a) Greek; (b) Medo-Persian; (c) Babylonian; (d) Roman empire is represented by the ten toes.

A Moment of Crisis

3

LESSON SCRIPTURE
Daniel 3

RELATED SCRIPTURE
Leviticus 26:1-39; Deuteronomy 4:9-31;
Revelation 13; 17

LESSON AIM
To refuse to compromise Scriptural
convictions.

LEARN BY HEART
"Be it known unto thee, O king, that we will
not serve thy gods, nor worship the golden
image which thou hast set up" (Daniel
3:18).

EVERY DAY WITH THE WORD

STUDENT'S NOTEBOOK

This column is for the student who desires additional study of the lesson theme.

Monday	The trial of a father	Genesis 22:1-18
Tuesday	The trial of a nation	Numbers 14:1-24
Wednesday	The trial of a leader	Judges 7:1-15
Thursday	The trial of a king	I Samuel 15:1-26
Friday	The trial of a prophet	I Kings 19:1-18
Saturday	The trial of the Lord	Matthew 4:1-11
Sunday	The trial of a believer	James 1:2-12

LESSON PREPARATION

Years ago there was a popular song alluding to many events which could make a hero out of the person who responded correctly to them. As each opportunity was examined, however, the response was always the same: "That's a fine opportunity for someone, for somebody else—not me." Thus every opportunity to become something more than ordinary was firmly rejected.

Doesn't this remind you of the average believer today? God brings experiences into his life which provide occasions for him to exhibit faith and courage, but he says, "Somebody else, Lord—not me." He seldom experiences the joy of a life walked by faith, and those around him are deprived of an example of the mighty works of God in response to faith. In this lesson, we study the excellent witness for God, which comes when God's power is coupled with man's obedience.

NEBUCHADNEZZAR'S DECREE
(Daniel 3:1-7)

This chapter opens with an account of Nebuchadnezzar's building a great golden image in the plain of Dura near the city of Babylon (Daniel 3:1). There is some doubt about what the image represented, but it probably was meant to impress the king's subjects with his majesty, might, and magnificence.

It may well have resembled one of his gods.

After the building of the image had been completed, the king commanded the governmental leaders of Babylon to attend its dedication (verse 2). Nebuchadnezzar was an absolute ruler; consequently, no one dared refuse his summons. Every governmental officer was represented (verse 3). One name is absent from the list—Daniel. Scripture is silent about the reason, but he may have been absent on extended business in some remote province of the empire.

God raised up Nebuchadnezzar and gave him imperial power. Now he sets out on a course to abuse that power by introducing idolatry.

The king then gave instructions concerning the procedure to be followed in the dedication. At the sound of the six musical instruments, the assembly of VIPs were to fall down and worship the image (verse 5). As an added inducement for the people to follow these instructions, the king commanded that those who did not obey were to be thrown into a hot furnace (verse 6). This must have eliminated from the minds of the people any thought of disobedience.

NEBUCHADNEZZAR'S DISCOVERY
(Daniel 3:8-18)

Daniel 3:8-18 makes it clear that there were three exceptions to this universal obedience. Daniel's three friends refused to bow. Evidently some of the Chaldeans were watching the Jews to see whether they would obey the king. When the three Jews failed to comply, the Chaldeans immediately went to the king and reported them (verse 8). It is doubtful that their main motivation was the threat the Jews presented to the authority of the king. It is more likely that the Chaldeans saw an opportunity to rid themselves of these foreign usurpers who had positions which, they felt, rightfully belonged to true Babylonians. Probably they had been looking for such an opportunity as this.

The men who accused the Jews were the very same men whom Daniel had rescued earlier from the wrath of the king. How ungrateful they were! Ingratitude is the sin of today's generation. See Romans 1:21; II Timothy 3:2.

After reminding the king of his decree (verses 9-11), they made three charges against the Jews: (1) they did not honor the king, (2) they would not worship the king's gods, and (3) they would not worship the golden image (verse 12). The reaction of the king was what they had hoped for: he was furious that anyone would defy him (verse 13).

The king considered this defiance a direct challenge to his authority, and this was conduct which he could not tolerate. Commanding that the three Jews be brought to him, he asked whether they understood the significance of what they had done (verse 14). Because he had no reason to question their loyalty in the past, and because they were such useful and wise servants, he gave them the benefit of the doubt by inquiring whether they had misunderstood the meaning of his decree. He gave them a second chance to worship the image. If they still disobeyed him, then their death was certain, for he boasted that no god could deliver them from his power (verse 15). The king could conceive of no power greater than what he himself or his gods exercised.

In chapter 2 Nebuchadnezzar learned about God's omniscience; he is about to learn of God's omnipotence.

The witness of the three Jews was loud and clear. They had no defense against the accusation made against them, for their disobedience was not caused by lack of understanding (verses 16-18). They knew worshiping the image meant a denial of the true God of Israel and an infraction of the first commandment (Exodus 20:3-5). They were willing to pay any price which the king might impose upon them. They realized that God could deliver them from the penalty decreed by the king, but they also considered the possibility that God might not choose to do so. Regardless of the outcome, they were determined to remain true to God. Their faith manifested itself by a willing submission to whatever God would allow to happen to them. In life or death, they could only gain through a faithful witness to God.

God does not always save us from the trial, but He always preserves us in it. See Hebrews 13:6.

NEBUCHADNEZZAR'S DISPOSITION
(Daniel 3:19-30)

The attitude expressed by the three Jews was

more than Nebuchadnezzar could endure. Their refusal to obey him and take advantage of his generous offer of a second chance compounded their guilt. They had challenged his authority, and now they insulted him. This made the king so angry that his physical appearance was changed (Daniel 3:19). No longer was he willing to give them an opportunity to repent. He had the furnace heated seven times hotter than necessary. It now matched the heat of his inflamed fury against the three Jews.

This furnace was something like a modern brick kiln. It was wider at the bottom than at the top and had two openings, one at the bottom where materials were added to supply the fire and where ashes were removed; the other, at the top where people were cast into the fire. A pair of steps led up the side of the furnace to the opening above.

After the fire was as hot as the king desired, he commanded that the three Jews be thrown down into the fire. The strongest men were appointed to this task because it required carrying the three Jews up the side of the furnace to the top (verse 20). The Jews were bound fully clothed, carried up to the top, and cast down right into the middle of the roaring flame (verses 21,23). The extremely high temperature of the fire is affirmed by what happened to the men who threw the Jews into the furnace. The heat and flames were so intense that they were scorched to death (verse 22). This helps illustrate the magnitude of the miracle which protected the intended victims.

Evidently Nebuchadnezzar was sitting near the furnace looking into the fire through the opening at the bottom. He expected to see three bodies

God's people have always been called upon to endure the ordeal of fire. See Isaiah 43:2; Malachi 3:2,3; I Peter 1:7; Revelation 3:18.

come crashing down, consumed by the fire in an instant. Imagine his surprise and shock when his expectations were disappointed. No wonder he left his seat and checked to see whether or not he could believe his eyes (verse 24). He asked his counselors to verify that the men had really been thrown into the fire. They confirmed the action.

Instead of three men the king saw four persons in the fire. The fourth person impressed the king as a supernatural being. In the original text verse 28 actually describes the fourth man as an angel or messenger of God. No further identification is given in this chapter, but we know that the being was either a preincarnate appearance of Christ or an angel sent by God to protect the three Jews. Another incredible detail was that the three men were no longer bound; they were freely walking around in the fire.

Other appearances of Christ in the Old Testament: Genesis 16:10; 18:1; Exodus 3:6; Joshua 5:14.

Nebuchadnezzar was convinced that the Jews had been delivered by supernatural means, and so he called the men to come out of the furnace. He calls them "servants of the most high God" (verse 26). Care must be taken not to read too much into the phrase. Nebuchadnezzar was a believer in polytheism. He admitted only that the God of the Jews was the greatest of all the gods. This is as far as he could go. It did not destroy his belief in his other gods, nor did he trust the Hebrews' God.

Having come out of the fire, the Jews were examined by the other governmental officials (verse 27). Here was manifest the full magnitude of the miracle. Nothing was burned; not even the smell of fire was on them! Their bodies and clothes were the same as before they entered the fire. As with all miracles that God performs, this miracle was complete in every detail.

The miracle being verified by all present, the king began to praise the God of the Jews. Two things impressed the king (verse 28). First, he observed the men's trust in God, which resulted in their deliverance. Second, he realized that they had completely yielded their bodies to God, although they knew it might cost them their lives. It would be dangerous to offend such a powerful God; therefore, the king made a decree forbidding anyone to speak against the God of the Jews (verse 29).

The king's final act was to reward the Jews. They were promoted in the governmental ranks of Babylon (verse 30). The occasion which threatened to destroy them provided instead for greater prominence in the kingdom. How frustrated their enemies must have been!

A crisis confronted the Jews; they faced the challenge courageously. These three men were found equal to the situation because they knew and trusted the God who is above every situation. Setting aside any thought of rationalization that would justify a compromise, they placed their confidence in God and stood their ground. As a result, they were privileged to hear a heathen dictator voicing his respect for God. God had visited the Gentiles with an unforgettable demonstration of His omnipotence, and they glorified the name of the most high God.

Chapter three contains more than a historical account of three courageous Jews. The chapter is reminiscent of the events of the tribulation. At the end of the times of the Gentiles, the man of sin will erect a statue in the temple at Jerusalem. He will order everyone to worship a Western dictator

Even the unsaved take notice of the believer's confidence in God. They cannot help admiring real courage when they see it.

See Esther 6:4-11.

Deuteronomy 31:6; Joshua 10:25; Psalm 27:14; Acts 28:15

Ephesians 6:13

God will be glorified by the heathen: Ezekiel 38:23; 39:7,21,23. See Psalm 2:8.

II Thessalonians 2:3,4; Matthew 24:15

Revelation 13:15

whom the statue represents. Death will be the penalty for defiance. Many Jews will die rather than to practice idolatry and worship the beast.

But God in His mercy will deliver thousands of saved Jews from their persecutors. He will protect them from the awful wrath of their enemies by hiding them in a place He has prepared to secure them until the tribulation judgments have passed. These Jews shall come through the fires refined and purified. In the day of Messiah's glory these saved Jewish survivors will be elevated to judicial and legislative positions in the administration of the coming kingdom of Christ on the earth. God shall be greatly glorified among the Gentiles as the result of His extraordinary work in the Israel of the future.

FOOD FOR THOUGHT

"Courage is the standing army of the soul which keeps it from conquest, pillage and slavery."
—Henry Van Dyke

Match the following:

1. The golden image was set up in the Babylonian plain of _____.
2. The image was _____ feet tall.
3. The religious ceremony was introduced by _____.
4. The furnace was _____ times its normal intensity.
5. The king saw _____ people walking around in the furnace.
6. The entire incident was a plot of the _____.
7. Nebuchadnezzar lauded the men's God because he was a _____.
8. The men suffered _____ harm.
9. _____ was not present at the ceremony.
10. _____ was with the men in the furnace.

a. no	g. Melzar	l. seven
b. Chaldeans	h. Daniel	m. minor
c. Jew	i. Christ	n. polytheist
d. Dura	j. king	o. four
e. fifteen	k. sixty	p. music
f. a meal		

Downfall of a Dictator

4

LESSON SCRIPTURE
Daniel 4

RELATED SCRIPTURE
II Chronicles 26:16-21; Proverbs
16:18-25; Isaiah 10:12-19; 28:1-13;
James 4:1-10

LESSON AIM
To humble ourselves before the Lord.

LEARN BY HEART
"Pride goeth before destruction, and an
haughty spirit before a fall" (Proverbs
16:18).

EVERY DAY WITH THE WORD

Monday	The fall of Satan	Isaiah 14:12-20
Tuesday	The fall of man	Genesis 3:1-7
Wednesday	The fall of a king	II Chronicles 26:16-23
Thursday	The fall of a nation	Isaiah 28:1-13
Friday	The fall of a city	Revelation 18
Saturday	The fall of a believer	James 4:1-10
Sunday	The cure for failure	Galatians 5:16-26

STUDENT'S NOTEBOOK

This column is for the student who desires additional study of the lesson theme.

LESSON PREPARATION

"Pride goeth. . . before a fall!" How many times have you heard this warning? Yet how frequently this sin of pride appears in the lives of men. The pathway of history is strewn with people who thought themselves self-sufficient and destined to lead others on to glory. The courts

Pride is the root of all wickedness. See Isaiah 14:9-17.

Genesis 3:5; Isaiah 14:14

are full of offenders whose troubles flow from pride. Many marital problems spring from the same source. Why is an almost universally condemned sin so prevalent and persistent a problem?

The absence of God from the life of a sinner leaves him wholly captivated by the selfish ego. The natural man is obsessed by his self-reliance, self-control, and self-esteem. In his pride he fancies himself a god and thus lives independently of God.

THE DANGER OF PRIDE
(Daniel 4:1-27)

This lesson deals with the subject of pride, the heights to which it soars, and the method which God uses to bring proud sinners to their knees. It magnifies God's absolute sovereignty and man's sinfulness. The account in the fourth chapter of Daniel was written by Nebuchadnezzar after he had learned about God's supremacy and mercy from a firsthand experience with the most high God.

I Kings 10:6,7; I John 1:1

The chapter is introduced by a brief prologue in which Nebuchadnezzar addresses all the subjects of his realm (verse 1). The king's jurisdiction encompassed a vast territory, and he wanted all of the peoples under his dominion to share the good news of his deliverance. Among other items, the announcement contains a proclamation of peace.

The Bible never covers up the sin of its characters but candidly and freely narrates both good and bad.

Ordinary men would have made every attempt to hide the fact that they had suffered a mental derangement, and certainly a universal monarch would not be eager for his subjects to learn of such a disgraceful debasement, but Nebuchadnezzar was determined that everyone should know about the "signs and wonders" which the God of Daniel had worked on the king's behalf (verse 2). He had had a personal transaction with the God of Heaven, and he was unashamed for his subjects to hear of it and benefit from it.

Nebuchadnezzar had come to understand something about the King and the kingdom eternal (verse 3). He was referring to God's absolute rule in all theaters of time and space, over all creatures—uninterrupred and universal.

The incident which the king is about to rehearse took place toward the close of his reign when relative peace had settled throughout the empire (verse 4). The Gentile world government had arrived at a status in which it was uncontested and unopposed. It had mounted up to lofty heights, glorious and powerful. Magnificence and majesty were everywhere displayed in the kingdom of Babylon.

The Oriental monarch's complacency was interrupted by a dream which disturbed his sleep and made him fearful of the future (verse 5). When his wise men could not interpret the dream, it was committed to Daniel (verse 9). The king describes the content of the dream in verses 10-17. He saw a tree planted on the earth and growing until it became so large that it stretched up to the skies and spread itself over all the earth. Its foliage was luxuriant and its fruit prolific. It afforded shelter for all the animals and birds who lived in its branches and received its provisions.

Then the king saw a supernatural being descending from Heaven—an angel who commanded the tree to be felled, the animals driven away, and the fruit scattered. The tree was not completely destroyed; a stump remained in the

Contrast Luke 21:26 with II Timothy 1:7.

Contrast this tree with the stone of Daniel 2:35.

ground. Fetters of iron and bronze were ordered for someone who was to be given the heart of a beast for the space of seven years and live like an animal of the field. The angel added that the fulfillment had been decreed and that it would serve God's purpose of vindicating His absolute sovereignty. Furthermore, it would demonstrate that God Himself elevates men to positions of earthly glory as it pleases Him and that He also deposes them at will (verse 17).

Matthew 13:31,32 implies that before the millennial kingdom is set up, men will find protection and provision in a counterfeit millennium—a kingdom of evil in which wicked man will repose (birds of carrion).

The tree represented Nebuchadnezzar in all his glory and grandeur (verses 20-22). Like the tree, he had exalted himself to Heaven, vaunting in his accomplishments; and like the tree, he had spread his dominion to the remote recesses of the world. Millions of people rested confidently in the protective shade of this "tree" and drew their sustenance from its provisions. The tree, then, includes both Nebuchadnezzar the emperor and the empire over which he ruled. It characterizes the first stage of Gentile world domination, and at the same time it illustrates the whole course of the Gentile period of supremacy until the last stage in the future tribulation.

An angel from Heaven sounds the death knell and calls for the hewing down of the tree just at the height of its glory (verse 23). The event spells the debasement of arrogant Nebuchadnezzar who imagined that he had gained his lofty position quite independently of God. At the same time it is a reminder of the coming collapse of the Babylonian empire (Daniel 5). Furthermore, it is indicative of the destruction of the last form of Gentile world power when God will bring the times of the Gentiles to a halt at the end of the tribulation.

Luke 21:24; Revelation 16:10; 18; 19:21

Daniel informed the king that he would suffer a seven-year period of insanity in which he would crawl about on all fours, fancying that he was an ox. He would be banished from the company of men and left to living with the brutes of the field, dieting on grass (verse 25). The band of iron and bronze probably means to suggest that the king will be fettered by madness—a mania from which he cannot escape until the duration of the decree expires.

The stump foretells that Nebuchadnezzar will survive the ordeal and live to be reinstated on the throne (verse 26). It implies also that the empire will outlive him and pass on to his successor. In addition, the cutting down of the tree speaks of the final destruction of Gentile rule at the end of the tribulation. The tribulation judgments will succeed in devastating the kingdom of the beast. All of his followers among the nations will be slain by the returning Messiah, but there will be survivors among the peoples of the earth. A group of saved Gentile survivors ("the stump") will emerge from the tribulation woes to enter the period of the millennial reign, when they will be the faithful subjects of King Jesus.

Daniel's parting word to the king is an appeal for him to forsake his sins and iniquities and prove that he has genuinely repented by producing deeds of kindness. Such a reversal of his attitudes and actions might avert the fulfillment of the prophecy and the judgment of God (verse 27).

DESTRUCTION OF PRIDE
(Daniel 4:28-37)

Evidently the dream, combined with Daniel's

Nebuchadnezzar lived like an animal even before his insanity, for like an animal he had no thought of God (II Peter 2:12; Jude 10).

Isaiah 10:19; Matthew 25:31-40; Revelation 7:9-17

Isaiah 11:10; Philippians 2:10

No sinner can stifle

the motions of the
flesh for long; they
soon erupt in worse
sins (II Peter
2:19-21).

Isaiah 10:13

God has absolute
control over the
mental processes
and can change
them at will. He
works in the minds of
believers especially
(Romans 12:2;
Ephesians 4:23), but
He also controls the
minds of the wicked
(Revelation 17:17).

plea, had a beneficial effect upon the king.
Nebuchadnezzar seems to have suppressed his
pride for about a year. But soon the dream faded
into forgetfulness and Daniel's warning went un-
heeded. The king fell back into his old haunts and
habits.

One day on the palace roof he was simply
overcome with a sense of his own greatness
(Daniel 4:29,30). He was surveying the vast city
of Babylon and was struck with the genius and
power by which he had attained such dizzying
heights. He framed his thoughts in words, and in
that moment the longsuffering of God ceased and
the threatened judgment fell (verse 31). The
period of opportunity and grace was past. The
king was to learn what a fearful thing it is to fall
into the hands of an angry God.

God withheld from Nebuchadnezzar his ra-
tional powers and reduced him to the level of the
irrational beast of the field (verse 33). This dem-
onstrates that God has direct access to the mental-
ity of men and that He can do with it anything that
suits His purpose. Nothing in Nebuchadnezzar's
succeeding actions is contrary to possibility. Med-
ical science has dealt with such aberrations for
centuries, and the general name by which such a
malady is defined is lycanthropy.

When the designated period had elapsed, God
restored the king's sanity. The first intimation of it
was the fact that he looked up to God (verse 34).
No beast looks up; they all point toward the turf,
for they have no consciousness of God. Only man
was created with a moral and religious nature, and
only man has the capacity to look to God for
forgiveness and for food. The protracted bestiality
was over, and Nebuchadnezzar lifted his voice in

an anthem of praise to God in His mercy.

The years of Nebuchadnezzar's beast-like conduct are vivid reminders again of the final stage of Gentile world power, for in the future the kingdoms of earth will be governed by two "beasts"—men who are savage and ferocious, energized by the devil and set on destroying the people of God. Power-crazed men will gladly accept the offer which the devil gave to Jesus to control the kingdoms of this world (Luke 4:5,6). Like the animals of the field they will entertain no thought of God. In utter godlessness and lawlessness they will exercise their jurisdiction over all the territory from the Atlantic to the Persian Gulf, and for all we know they will extend their territorial sway to worldwide proportions. But they will be brought down to the pit, and the unexcelled magnificence of their empire will be reduced to rubble in an hour.

The beast out of the sea (Revelation 13:1) will control Western Europe, and the beast out of the earth (verse 11) will control the Middle East. Between them they will share world supremacy.

Nebuchadnezzar learned much from his experience (Daniel 4:35-37). He knew that there existed only one eternal God—the most High. He knew that God was supreme and all-glorious and that he would not share his glory with the creature. He knew that men are as nothing in God's sight. Man has absolutely nothing with which to commend himself to God; all his works are worthless and transitory. He learned that God has the right to do exactly as He pleases without consulting the creature first or ever. God's sovereignty extends to the highest Heaven and to the lowest Hell. Nothing in Heaven above or on the earth below can thwart God's purposes or interrupt His plans. Nebuchadnezzar learned that no mortal man has the right to question what God does. God acts in unfettered liberty to do with His creatures any-

Deuteronomy 6:4

Isaiah 42:8

Job 42:6; Psalm 8:4

Ephesians 1:11

thing He pleases, and the creature only shows his insolence and rebellion and pride when he reacts against God's ways or when he takes upon himself prerogatives which belong only to God. The king learned that God is eternally just and true, faithful and righteous altogether. Do we believe these same truths?

FOOD FOR THOUGHT

"God's ways are behind the scenes, but He moves all the scenes which He is behind."
—J. N. Darby

NOW TEST YOUR KNOWLEDGE

Answer true or false:
1. Daniel 4 emphasizes God's love.
2. Daniel 4 was written by Nebuchadnezzar.
3. Nebuchadnezzar kept his experience a secret.
4. The events of Daniel 4 occurred at the beginning of Nebuchadnezzar's reign.
5. Nebuchadnezzar's illness was mental.
6. The immense tree was a picture of Heaven.
7. The Gentile empire of the future will be headed up by two beasts.
8. An angel will announce the destruction of the Babylon of the future.
9. Nebuchadnezzar's seven years of insanity remind us of the seven-year millennium.

Collapse of
a Kingdom

LESSON SCRIPTURE
Daniel 5

RELATED SCRIPTURE
Isaiah 13; 14:18-27; Jeremiah 50; 51

LESSON AIM
To trust in the Lord, not in worldly
possessions.

LEARN BY HEART
"And I will render unto Babylon and to all
the inhabitants of Chaldea all their evil that
they have done in Zion in your sight, saith
the Lord" (Jeremiah 51:24).

EVERY DAY WITH THE WORD

Monday	The beginning of Babylon	Genesis 10:1-10
Tuesday	Babylon's first revolt	Genesis 11:1-9
Wednesday	God's use of Babylon foretold	Jeremiah 21
Thursday	God's use of Babylon realized	II Kings 25:1-24
Friday	God's judgment on Babylon	Isaiah 47
Saturday	Babylon's final revolt	Revelation 17
Sunday	Babylon's final destruction	Revelation 18

STUDENT'S NOTEBOOK

This column is for the
student who desires
additional study of
the lesson theme.

LESSON PREPARATION

Overjoyed with a handful of her own money, a
little girl entered the discount store to buy some

trinket that would increase her delight. Her eyes fixed upon some gold-colored chains. How they sparkled! She purchased one of them and went merrily on her way. But only a few weeks later she looked with sad and tearful eyes at her beloved chain. Its gold color had disappeared, leaving only a dull, unattractive, worthless piece of metal. She had learned that outward appearance is not always representative of the actual worth.

Our inheritance in Heaven "fadeth not away" (I Peter 1:4).

This is an accurate appraisal of Babylon at the time the events of Daniel 5 occurred. Although there was an outward appearance of prosperity and security, the armies of the Medo-Persians were beating at the city gates, and great Babylon was soon to fall in fulfillment of Daniel's prophecy in chapter 2.

A PROFANE ORGY
(Daniel 5:1-16)

For hundreds of years Daniel 5 was the only literary source for the fact of Belshazzar's reign. No other document of antiquity mentioned Belshazzar. The ancient records seemed to contradict Daniel by stating that Nabonidus was the last king of the Babylonian empire. Naturally the destructive critics made much of this apparent discrepancy and pointed to Daniel as a first-class example of unreliability.

Babylonian records give his name as "Belsharusur" meaning "Bel, protect the king."

In more recent times, however, the accuracy of Daniel has been verified by archaeological discoveries. Belshazzar's name has appeared on Babylonian inscriptions, and we now know that he reigned in Babylon while Nabonidus was absent from the city. Belshazzar was the eldest son of Nabonidus, and reigned concurrently with him.

On October 29, 539 B.C., Belshazzar entertained the aristocracy of Babylon at a most unusual feast. It was unparalleled for the presence and numbers of dignitaries (verse 1), for drunkenness (verse 2), for desecration (verse 3), and for defiance (verse 4). In all the annals of Biblical history Belshazzar's banquet is unrivaled for debauchery, blasphemy, revelry, and profanity. He provided a menu of wine, women, and wantonness. The presence of women (wives and concubines) added to the unexampled character of the occasion, for women were rarely invited to this kind of feast (Esther 1:10-12).

But Belshazzar was not satisfied until he had committed a terrible sacrilege. Inflamed with wine, he decided to do something daring and sensational. He would mock the living God by defiling the sacred utensils which his grandfather had removed from the Temple at Jerusalem. To show the superiority of the Babylonian gods, he commanded that the golden and silver vessels be filled with wine and distributed to his intoxicated guests.

The Tabernacle furnishings were not to be defiled by unsuitable hands (I Samuel 5:8-12; II Samuel 6:6,7).

One other motive may have sparked the feast and suggested the profanation of the holy vessels. For weeks the armies of Medo-Persia, under the command of Cyrus and Darius, had been engaged in a campaign against Babylon, with no results. The Babylonians were entrenched behind the impregnable walls of the city with rations to last them almost indefinitely. Belshazzar believed that his heathen deities had secured him against the seige of Cyrus and the eastern army, and so the king arranged a feast to honor his gods and to show his contempt for the Medes and Persians.

Belshazzar should have been fasting not feasting. His life and kingdom were at stake, and yet he rested in a false confidence. See I Thessalonians 5:3 and Isaiah 28:15-20.

Belshazzar felt so invulnerable inside his mighty fortifications that he gave vent to an utter reckless abandon.

In the grim watches of the night when the orgy had reached its dizzy height, the fingers of a man's hand, writing on the palace wall, brought the wicked merrimakers to a sudden and sober halt. The king was so affected by the mysterious interruption that his face turned to a ghastly pallor, his mind reeled under the force of it, and his knees trembled uncontrollably (Daniel 5:6). His own guilty conscience told him that he could not expect anything but bad news from Heaven.

Experience, conscience, nature and history are powerless to transform men. Only the Holy Spirit is sufficient for this.

Charlatans filled the palace, and although Nebuchadnezzar had thoroughly exposed their incompetence and fraudulence, Belshazzar had learned nothing from the past. So he summoned the wise men to interpret the cryptogram, with a promise to elevate anyone who succeeded to the third place in the kingdom (verse 7). But the efforts of the wise men proved as futile as they were in Nebuchadnezzar's day, and the king despaired of solving the riddle (verses 8,9).

Then Nebuchadnezzar's widow came to the banquet hall, counseling her grandson to appeal to Daniel. She gave a resume of Daniel's character, position, and superhuman knowledge (verses 10-12).

If Daniel was in his late teens when he was taken captive, he would be about 90 years old at the death of Belshazzar.

Daniel, now an old man, must have been rudely awakened from his peaceful slumbers and brought before the king with all haste. Belshazzar commenced his interview with Daniel by a confirmation of his pedigree (verses 13,14), continued with a presentation of the problem (verse 15), and concluded with a promise to reward Daniel with prestige, power, and a princedom (verse 16).

A PROPHETIC ORACLE
(Daniel 5:17-30)

Daniel's first response was to refuse the gifts of the profligate king (Daniel 5:17). He could not be bribed or bought, and he did not read the divine inscription for money. Daniel knew that the treasures and glory of Babylon were no longer Belshazzar's to give; soon they would be the possessions of Cyrus.

II Kings 5:5,16,20-27; Acts 3:6; 8:20

Isaiah 45:1-4

Thereupon, Daniel recounted to Belshazzar God's dealings with Nebuchadnezzar. In His providence God had raised Nebuchadnezzar up to irresistible might and authority; He had delegated to him absolute control over the affairs of nations (verses 18,19). But Nebuchadnezzar abused his power and acted toward God in insolence and obstinacy with the result that the Lord denied him his reason, dethroned him, and debased him (verses 20,21).

Genesis 9:1-7; Romans 13:1-7; I Peter 2:13-16; Revelation 17:17

Then, before Daniel deciphered the enigma and declared the doom of the young king, he commented on Belshazzar's crime. His impudence was worse even than Nebuchadnezzar's. He had insulted God Himself by profaning the consecrated instruments of His sanctuary, by exalting himself above God, by refusing to acknowledge his dependence upon God, by denying God's supremacy, and by robbing God of the glory due His name. Man's first responsibility is to glorify God, but Belshazzar glorified the gods of Babylon and defied the God of Heaven (verses 22,23).

Romans 1:18-23

Lucifer illustrates pride against God (Isaiah 14:12-17).

God's patience exhausted, righteous judgment must be executed. The day of reckoning had

Jeremiah 27:6,7

Isaiah 13:3,17;
21:2; 41:2,25;
Daniel 11:44
Revelation 16:12

In Zechariah 5:5-11
"Shinar" refers to
Babylon of the
future.

dawned, and Daniel pronounced the sentence of doom in the interpretation of the writing. "Mene"—the allotted number of days for the duration of the Babylonian empire had been determined by God, and they had run their course. "Tekel"—Belshazzar had been weighed in the scale of God's standard and been found too light to qualify. "Upharsin"—the kingdom had already been taken from him and given to the Medes and Persians (verses 24-28).

Belshazzar kept his word to Daniel and promoted him to become the third ruler in the kingdom, but the king did not live long enough to see Daniel installed. Before the light of morning had broken across the eastern skies, Cyrus' soldiers entered the city by marching under the walls in the muddy river-bed of the Euphrates, and Belshazzar came to an ignominious end.

Daniel 5 involves more than what merely meets the eye. It is, on the surface, a history of the collapse of the Babylonian empire of the past, but it is also a forecast of the destruction of great Babylon of the future. The whole book of Daniel was written with the times of the Gentiles in view—their commencement, course, characteristics, culmination, and collapse. Everything which is true of the early stages of the Gentile period of world politics is also true of the final stage of Gentile history. The initial stage and the ultimate stage are both marked by the prominence of ruling classes, commerce, covetousness, concubines, carousals, contempt for God, consternation, and condemnation.

FOOD FOR THOUGHT

"We shall only be judged by what we know; but if we know, then we are guilty if we do not do."
—Guy R. King

NOW TEST YOUR KNOWLEDGE

Choose the correct answers:
1. Babylon was experiencing great (a) spiritual revival; (b) moral decay; (c) territorial expansion.
2. Daniel was about (a) ninety; (b) fifty; (c) thirty.
3. Babylon (a) tolerated; (b) forbade; (c) preferred sensual living.
4. The vessels Belshazzar desecrated were from the temple at (a) Rome; (b) Alexandria; (c) Jerusalem.
5. When he saw the writing on the wall, Belshazzar (a) railed against God; (b) became angry; (c) trembled.
6. Belshazzar would make the interpreter of the words (a) the highest; (b) the second; (c) the third ruler in the land.
7. Belshazzar (a) ignored; (b) accepted; (c) did not know the lesson God taught Nebuchadnezzar.
8. God told Belshazzar that his kingdom was (a) extended; (b) suspended; (c) ended.
9. The Babylonian empire would be conquered by (a) Rome; (b) Medo-Persia; (c) Greece.
10. The fulfillment of the words on the wall took place (a) the following year; (b) immediately; (c) after Belshazzar's son became king.

The Plot That Failed

6

LESSON SCRIPTURE
Daniel 6

RELATED SCRIPTURE
Genesis 37—45; Isaiah 44:24—45:4;
Jeremiah 30:1-9; Matthew 27; John
20:1-18

LESSON AIM
To have a regular, active prayer life.

LEARN BY HEART
"That ye may be blameless and harmless,
the sons of God, without rebuke, in the
midst of a crooked and perverse nation,
among whom ye shine as lights in the
world" (Philippians 2:15).

STUDENT'S NOTEBOOK

This column is for the student who desires additional study of the lesson theme.

EVERY DAY WITH THE WORD

Monday	The prayer of intercession	Genesis 18:23-33
Tuesday	The prayer for guidance	Genesis 24:12-21
Wednesday	The prayer for wisdom	I Kings 3:1-13
Thursday	The prayer for protection	Nehemiah 4:1-12
Friday	The prayer for healing	Matthew 8:1-13
Saturday	The prayer for mercy	Matthew 15:21-28
Sunday	The prayer of thanks	Ephesians 1:15-23

LESSON PREPARATION

In a day of political intrigue, governmental graft, and credibility gaps, it is refreshing to review the integrity of Daniel, whose only "fault" was a godly life and conscientious business dealings.

The circumstances were certainly extenuating, for Daniel was an old man, long overdue for retirement; he was all alone in a corrupt culture and court. He was hated by his associates and under continual surveillance. How will he react to adversity? Will he "be able to withstand in the evil day, and having done all, to stand"?

Ephesians 6:13

THE HISTORIC INCIDENT
(Daniel 6)

Darius the Mede advanced the aged Daniel to a very prominent and influential position in the Persian government (Daniel 6:1-3). We are not informed about what led to Daniel's promotion, but we may surmise that his long familiarity with the intricacies of administration would make him a valuable asset to the new regime. Darius may have heard of Daniel's ministries to Nebuchadnezzar and Belshazzar. He had doubtlessly come to realize that Daniel could be depended upon to manage well the affairs of state.

Other servants of the Lord held governmental positions: Joseph—Genesis 41:41-43; Esther—Esther 2:17; Mordecai—Esther 10:3; Nehemiah—Nehemiah 2:1. Do you know modern politicians who are Christians?

But the elevation of this Jew to such heights of service and honor won him the hatred of envious politicians who determined to bring an indictment against the prophet and thus remove him from office (verse 4). By their own admission, Daniel's private and public life was flawless, and so they plotted to impeach him by leveling charges against him concerning his religious devotion (verse 5). Appealing to Darius' vanity and implying that Darius himself was a god, the conspirators enticed the king to pass a law forbidding prayers to any other god for a period of thirty days (verses 6-9). They counted on Daniel's defying the irrevocable Persian decree, and they were not

Read Esther 6.

I Timothy 3:7

Daniel prayed privately—"in his chamber"; unashamedly— "windows being open"; reverently—"three times a day"; gratefully—"gave thanks"; and regularly—"as he did aforetime."

disappointed. According to his custom, Daniel faced toward Jerusalem and knelt in prayer to his God three times a day (verse 10).

The rogues detected Daniel's infraction of the law and reported it to the king (verses 11-13). Darius realized too late that he had been tricked into setting his signature to the diabolical edict. He was bent upon finding some loophole in the law, but the law was binding (verses 14,15). Darius had no alternative except to carry out the demands of the law by casting Daniel into the den of lions (verses 16,17).

As soon as it was daybreak, Darius hastened to the execution chamber to inspect the result (verse 19). He was delighted to find Daniel unharmed (verses 20-23). Daniel was removed from the den, and the men who plotted his destruction were fed to the lions (verses 23,24). The king celebrated the occasion by sending a peace proclamation into the whole realm exalting Daniel's living, faithful and eternal God (verses 25-27).

THE TYPICAL IMPORT

Daniel in the lion's den is nowhere in Scripture called a type, but the details of this chapter are so minutely repeated in the life, death, and resurrection of Jesus Christ that it is impossible not to see the relationship here.

Daniel was one of a triumvirate whom Darius intended to set over the whole realm (Daniel 6:2,3). Christ is one of the three persons of the triune Godhead whom the Father intends will govern the whole world in the day of His millennial glory. Daniel's character was spotless; he was motivated by an indwelling spirit (verse 3). Christ

Psalm 2:6-12

47

was innocent and sinless. His whole life from birth to resurrection was under the absolute control of the Holy Spirit.

Daniel's holy life was such a daily rebuke to the indiscretions and irregularities of the heads of state that they trumped up charges against him and got a conviction on the grounds of his relationship to his God. The rulers of the Jewish people were so filled with envy against Christ that they schemed to kill Him by charging Him with blasphemy—claiming to be equal with God.

Daniel was condemned by an unchanging law (verse 8). The unalterable law of God was involved in the death of Christ. The law said: ''The soul that sinneth, it shall die.'' Christ was sinless, but He was taking the place of those who had broken the holy law of God. He came to satisfy the just demands of the law in the stead of transgressors of that law.

Before Daniel's execution day he faced toward the holy city and prayed (verse 10). Before the day of crucifixion Jesus set His face toward Jerusalem and agonized in prayer in the garden of Gethsemane. Darius wanted to save Daniel, but he could not set aside the law (verses 14,15). Pilate believed in Christ's innocence and attempted to set Him free but could not.

Daniel was cast into the place of death and a stone, sealed with the signet of a Gentile empire, secured the entrance (verses 16,17). Christ went to the place of a skull and poured out His life in violent death. He was taken down from the cross and placed in a sepulcher sealed with the Gentile insignia and secured by Roman guards.

Very early in the day, a mourning king hurried to the intended sepulcher to inquire of Daniel's

Even Jesus' enemies testified to His sinlessness: Matthew 27:4,19; Luke 23:41,47; see Isaiah 53:9.

John 5:18

Ezekiel 18:4
Isaiah 53:5,6

Matthew 20:18; 23:37

John 19:4

Matthew 27:62-66

John 20:1-17

condition (verses 19,20). As it began to dawn on Sunday, mourning women came to Joseph's tomb to prepare the body of Jesus for permanent burial. The king, to his utter amazement, heard the "dead" Daniel speak (verses 21,22). Mary, at the garden tomb, heard her beloved Master speak to her. Angels attended Daniel's deliverance (verse 22), and angels figured prominently in announcing the resurrection of Christ.

Daniel was rescued from the place of certain death without so much as a scratch upon him (verse 23). Christ came from the tomb in resurrection glory, having defeated death and the grave. Daniel fulfilled every requirement of the law; nevertheless, he lived. The Persian law demanded only that he be thrown into the den of lions. The law did not specify that the lions must eat him, and it did not say that he had to remain in the lion's lair. Christ satisfied completely the offended holiness of God and fulfilled perfectly the broken law of God by dying the sinner's death; and yet He lives. The law did not require that He remain dead or that the grave hold its prey indefinitely. He met the demands of the law and lived despite the legal infliction of death. Sinners could not die as a penalty for their sins and live, too, but the God-Man "was delivered for our offences, and was raised again for our justification."

Daniel's deliverance from the jaws of death was occasioned by the universal promulgation of a message of peace (verse 25). Christ has made peace for us through the blood of His cross. We are preaching the gospel of peace. The ambassadors of Christ are calling upon all men everywhere to be reconciled to God (be at peace with God). The content of the proclamation in-

Revelation 1:18

Galatians 3:13; 4:4,5

Hebrews 7:25

Romans 4:25

Romans 5:1;
Colossians 1:20

cluded a message of life—"the living God" (verse 26). One special ingredient of the gospel message is the news about a living Saviour— "and that he arose again the third day" (I Corinthians 15:4).

In the historic incident the law was satisfied (Daniel 6:16), God was glorified (verse 26), and Daniel was magnified, for his name accompanied every report of the miracle (verse 27). In the antitype, the law was satisfied, God was glorified, Christ was magnified, and sinners were justified on the basis of Christ's redeeming work. The inexorable demands of the law could no longer claim the offending sinner.

An "antitype" is the type fulfilled.

THE PROPHETIC IMPLICATION

Every isolated historic event recorded in the Bible has some indispensable connection with God's overall plan and purpose to inaugurate the coming kingdom. Scripture records only that history which has some bearing upon the ultimate goal of history.

Learn to study these passages from the viewpoint of their typical, practical, evangelical, prophetic, biographical, historical, and theological value.

In some ways Darius was a kind man— although certainly weak and largely controlled by his own officials. But what he did has prophetic significance irrespective of his personal traits, for his conduct conforms exactly to what will happen in the tribulation of the future. Darius arrogated to himself prerogatives which belong only to God (Daniel 6:7). He set himself up as God and forbade his subjects to petition anyone except himself for thirty days. His blasphemy will be repeated by the final oppressor of God's elect people in the tribulation; he will exalt himself above all that is called God.

Revelation 20:4

Revelation 6:9-11

Revelation 7:1-8

Revelation 15:2

Revelation 19:20

In the period of the tribulation many saved Jews will refuse to acknowledge the beast's authority; and, like Daniel, this remnant of believing Jews will suffer the consequences of their devotion to God. Many of them will feel the pain of death for this faith in Jesus. But God will spare many, delivering them as He did Daniel. They will be preserved from martyrdom by the intervening hand of God. Just as Daniel was faced by wild beasts and was rescued, so the Jewish remnant will face the ferocity of the two beasts of Revelation and get the victory over them.

The same deification of man mentioned in the Babylonian empire (Daniel 2) appeared also in the Medo-Persian empire (chapter 6). This principle later erupted in the Greek empire under the blasphemous conduct of Antiochus Epiphanes and again in the Roman empire under the Caesars. It characterizes the times of the Gentiles from beginning to end; and in the coming finale of Gentile dominion, the deification of man will be reintroduced in the person of the beast and in his false prophet. But just as Daniel's foes were cast to their doom in the pit of lions, the enemies of Israel in the tribulation will be cast alive into the lake of fire, which is the second death.

The events which followed Daniel's deliverance are all reminders of conditions which will prevail during the age to come. Darius sent out a peace proclamation which had a universal scope (verse 25). In the millennial kingdom the peoples of the earth will live in peace at last. Peace will come not only to men but to animals. Men shall learn war no more, and beasts shall lose their ferocity. In that day men will be reconciled to God and live in harmony with His laws.

Darius' subjects were under obligation to render proper respect and reverence to the God of Daniel (verse 26). During the kingdom reign of Christ, every knee shall bow and every tongue will confess that He is Lord to the glory of the Father. The Gentiles will come to a knowledge of the Lord, and they will be subservient to Israel.

Philppians 2:10,11

The kingdom which Darius envisioned was an everlasting kingdom. He doubtless spoke more than he knew, for the coming kingdom of the Messiah will endure as long as earth remains. The kingdom of God will come at last to earth, and it will never again be jeopardized by human defiance of divine authority.

FOOD FOR THOUGHT

"I hope I shall always possess firmness and virtue enough to maintain what I consider the most enviable of all titles, the character of an honest man."

—George Washington

NOW TEST YOUR KNOWLEDGE

Answer true or false:

1. Daniel was a teenager when Darius was king.
2. Daniel's co-workers accidentally implicated him in the matter of praying.
3. Darius' pride was the original cause of his edict.
4. Daniel prayed twice a week.
5. Daniel prayed facing Jerusalem.
6. Darius' hatred for Daniel caused him to be unflinching in meting out punishment.
7. Daniel is a type of the body of Christ.
8. Like Daniel, Christ was unjustly accused and punished.
9. God miraculously brought Daniel back to life after the lions killed him.
10. Darius refused to believe in Daniel's God.

The Rise of the Western Dictator

7

LESSON SCRIPTURE
Daniel 7

RELATED SCRIPTURE
Revelation 11:7; 13:1-10; 15:2;
16:2,10,13; 17; 19:19,20; 20:10

LESSON AIM
To live righteously, realizing that God is
sovereign.

LEARN BY HEART
"And the kingdom and dominion, and the
greatness of the kingdom under the whole
heaven, shall be given to the people of the
saints of the most High, whose kingdom is
an everlasting kingdom, and all dominions
shall serve and obey him" (Daniel 7:27).

EVERY DAY WITH THE WORD

Monday	Preaching the kingdom	Matthew 3:1-12
Tuesday	Saints in the kingdom	Matthew 5:1-12
Wednesday	A foreglimpse of the kingdom	Matthew 17:1-3
Thursday	Qualifications for the king	Matthew 18:1-14
Friday	The delay of the kingdom	Matthew 22:1-14
Saturday	Signs of the kingdom	Matthew 24:1-14
Sunday	The joy of the kingdom	Matthew 25:14-23

STUDENT'S NOTEBOOK

This column is for the
student who desires
additional study of
the lesson theme.

LESSON PREPARATION

The evolutionary interpretation of human history sees it as a gradual rise from brutes and
barbarism to a more and more advanced level of

The Bible says that wicked men will become worse and worse and that lawlessness will increase (II Timothy 3:13).

civilization and culture. Generally, the outlook is associated with the doctrine of perfectibility and inevitable progress. This philosophy places no limitations on the glorious heights to which man can and will ascend.

The Biblical analysis of man's history is just the opposite. The Scripture narrates man's noble and perfect beginning and then proceeds to trace his descent from society with God to savagery. Technologically, man has accomplished almost miracles; spiritually and ethically, he has been in retrogression since the fatal transgression in Eden.

The subject at hand gives us a glimpse of the end product—the final stage of man's swift downward plunge to bestiality and the ultimate in moral degradation.

THE CONTENT OF THE DREAM
(Daniel 7:1-14)

Belshazzar began to act as co-regent with his father about the year 553 B.C.

Chapter 7 turns the clock back to the accession year of Belshazzar (verse 1) when Daniel was granted a series of divine revelations which came to him through the medium of dreams and visions. Not everything which Daniel saw in visionary form is recorded in detail; he wrote down only the salient features of their content—a kind of summary with special attention given to world kingdoms. Actually, the content of chapter 7 consists of four visions: (1) the vision of the three beasts; (2) the vision of the fourth beast; (3) the vision of the judgment scene; and (4) the vision of the coming of the Son of Man.

First, Daniel saw a terrible tempest unleashed

upon the area of the great sea (verse 2). "The four winds" suggest all the directions of the compass. Violent agitation concentrates upon those territories bordering on the Mediterranean Sea. The angels who are responsible for restraining universal commotion and catastrophe (Revelation 7:1) permit the storms to rage uncontrollably.

Zechariah 6:5; Jeremiah 49:36

Evil angels have some kind of control over the empires of earth (Daniel 10:13; Ephesians 6:12).

Out of the surging, billowing waters arose four tremendous monsters, each different from the other (Daniel 7:3). Daniel described each as it appeared beginning with a lion (verse 4), continuing with a bear and a leopard (verses 5,6), and concluding with the mention of a beast so ferocious and unique that Daniel could compare it with no known creature (verse 7). It had iron teeth and ten horns. In contemplating the ten horns, Daniel noticed the rise of an eleventh horn, occasioned by the uprooting of three of the other horns (verse 8).

Then the prophet's eye beheld a governmental scene in Heaven (verse 9). Seats were arranged around a central throne on which sat the Ancient of days. The very same description in Revelation 1 is given of Christ, although here in Daniel God the Father is in view. He is the chief justice who decides the affairs of men and earth. "Ancient" intimates the eternity of the divine person. The white hair is an emblem of purity and holiness. The fiery flame and burning wheels, reminiscent of Ezekiel 1, are indicative of severity. The fiery stream speaks of the going forth of judgment in which sinners are consumed (Daniel 7:10).

The 100 million spirit beings who stand ministering before Him are angels and should be distinguished from the occupants of the lesser thrones (verses 9,10). Expositors are divided in their opin-

Compare Ezekiel 1:5-14 with Revelation 4:6-8.

ion of whether the lesser thrones are occupied by a different order of spirit beings or by human representatives of Israel or of the church.

At any rate, the sovereign of the universe has decided to judge earth dwellers for their awful wickedness. This should not be confused with the great white throne judgment after the millennial reign. The judgment in Daniel 7 occurs before the millennial kingdom and especially concerns the destiny of the fourth beast (verse 11). The judgment proceeds on the basis of what was recorded in the books. The deeds of men are written down for evidence against them. God's righteous judgment will not overlook the works which men have done.

In a final vision, Daniel sees the Son of man coming with the clouds of heaven (verse 13). This is a revelation of Christ with special emphasis upon His humanity, His relationship to Israel as the Messiah, and His role as the governor of nations (verse 14). Christ has proved Himself eminently qualified to rule, as every other human representative has not, and now He is invested with universal regal authority.

Daniel describes both the king and the kingdom. The scope of the kingdom will include "all peoples, nations and languages." The kingdom is as enduring as the earth itself. The kingdom, then, refers to the future worldwide sway of Jesus Christ over the governments of earth. None will contest His authority and none will dethrone the king of glory. The kingdom here in Daniel is the earthly millennial kingdom, the restored Davidic kingdom, the Messianic kingdom and not the universal sovereignty of God—sometimes called the absolute kingdom—which He has always exer-

Several books seem to be kept in Heaven: the book of the living (Psalm 68:28); book of life (Philippians 4:3; Revelation 3:5; 20:12,15); book of remembrance (Malachi 3:16); and book of works (Revelation 10:12).

There can be no kingdom without the king. As long as the king is rejected and absent from earth, the kingdom will be delayed. Some teachers speak of the postponement of the kingdom. They mean the interval during which the kingdom program has been suspended

cised in the affairs of men. The millennial age is a future period in history during which the universal government of God will be exercised on earth without opposition from men, through a human mediator—the man Christ Jesus.

(during the church age).

THE CLARIFICATION OF THE DREAM (Daniel 7:15-28)

The visions were entirely beyond Daniel's ability to interpret. He had gazed upon some terrible scenes, and his spirit was disquieted (Daniel 7:15). An angel imparted the information Daniel sought (verse 16).

The beasts represent the successive empires of ancient Babylon (lion) Medo-Persia (bear), Greece (leopard), and Rome (the nondescript beast), especially at the time when these empires extended their dominions to include the Mediterranean coasts. The beasts do not seem to describe the initial beginnings of these empires so much as a later stage in their development.

In chapter 2 we have the same succession where Nebuchadnezzar sees the outward glory of empires. But here in chapter 7 God sees the same empires as untamed jungle beasts ready to pounce and pulverize.

When it comes to the fourth beast, we have something that goes way beyond anything that ever developed in the ancient Roman empire. When Daniel sees this beast, it not only dominates the world of the Mediterranean but exists in the form of a ten-state unification. The angel interprets the horns to be "ten kings that shall arise" (verse 24). It cannot mean that they will come on the scene successively, one after the other with perhaps long intervals between. They are all ruling simultaneously when an eleventh king puts in his appearance. Never in the past was the Roman empire ruled by ten contemporaneous kings.

"The great sea" might just represent the unsettled state of the masses (Isaiah 17:12; Revelation 17:15).

The ten horns are identical in meaning to the ten

toes of the image in Nebuchadnezzar's dream. The ten horns, like the ten toes, represent a future development in which the Mediterranean world will be controlled by ten united states. This form of government will be functioning when Christ returns from glory to destroy it. The fourth kingdom, in this ten-nation form, will be the last Gentile world government and will be demolished to make room for the fifth world government—a theocracy under the rule of the Messiah (verses 14,18,22,27).

The kingdom of Messiah did not follow the collapse of Rome in A.D. 476, and the Roman empire at that time was not ruled by ten kings simultaneously. The fourth beast is ancient Rome, but the stage of the empire, as Daniel describes it, belongs to the future tribulation period.

Most of Daniel 7 deals with the fourth kingdom, the ten horns, and the little horn because these are the matters which have special significance for the time of the end. The first three beasts get little consideration because they do not have future ramifications—except that the territories of Babylon, Persia, and Greece were conquered by ancient Rome and will be included in the territories of the reorganized Roman empire. Moreover, the future empire will be characterized by the voracity of Babylon, the tenacity of Persia, the velocity of Greece, and the rapacity of Rome.

The little horn must now engage our interest. After the ten kings have asserted their authority over the vast empire of the future, another king will make his appearance. He has an insignificant arrival—"little horn," but he soon makes his authority felt. He overcomes opposition from

Although these kingdoms are historical and successive in their rising, one does not completely destroy the other. Each continues in its characteristic features until they are all combined in the reorganized empire of the future.

Five of these kings may preside over Europe and the other five over the Middle East.

three kings and is catapulted to absolute sovereignty over the reorganized empire (verse 24). He is especially remarkable for diabolical intelligence (verses 8,20). His eyes mesmerize his audiences. He is a master of persuasive oratory. Primarily his verbal abuse is directed against the most high God and the tribulation saints (verse 25). His dictatorship will continue for three and one-half years—the last half of the seven-year tribulation.

Do not be surprised to find the title "antichrist" sometimes applied to this little horn, for many Bible teachers use the term "antichrist" to identify the first beast of Revelation 13:1-10. But the writer of this course follows the Scofield view which reserves the title "antichrist" for the second beast of Revelation 13:11-18. All premillennial interpreters agree that the first beast of Revelation and the little horn of Daniel 7 are one and the same person, but not all agree to which end-time personality the title "antichrist" should be applied.

Getting these end-time characters distinguished and identified is one of the most complicated projects in prophetic studies. The view of the *Scofield Reference Bible* is most helpful. It distinguishes the Jewish antichrist (the beast out of the earth, the false prophet) from the little horn of Daniel 7 (the prince that shall come of Daniel 9:26, the beast out of the sea). It seems most in keeping with the full picture of Scripture to take the view that the antichrist is the last ecclesiastical head of the reorganized Roman empire, and the European dictator is the last civil head. We shall learn about the Jewish antichrist more in detail in lesson 12.

The saints of verses 18,21,22,25,27 are people who will be saved after the church saints have been raptured. Many of the saints of the tribulation period will survive the judgments and remain on the earth after the tribulation to become the citizens of the millennial kingdom.

The interpretation presented here of these end-time prophecies is also held by such well-known Bible teachers and writers as Ironside, Gaebelein, Tatford, Tatham, James Scott, Walter Scott, Darby, Kelly, W. E. Rogers and others. In this view, the beast-emperor of

Europe is the antigod. The false prophet is the antichrist. Satan (the dragon) is the antispirit who energizes them. We have, then, an unholy trinity of evil (Revelation 16:13).

Revelation 13:1-10 gives the clearest analysis of the character and conduct of the little horn of Daniel 7—the European beast-dictator. In all of its details this passage corresponds to what Daniel discloses. In vision John sees a beast rise out of the Mediterranean Sea—a beast which already has ten horns (verse 1). The empire of the future is a composite of the leopard, bear, and lion (verse 2), which suggests that the empire of the beast will eventually incorporate everything within the old territories. The empire of the future will be brought out of a period of inactivity and rise to political supremacy (verse 3). The emperor will demand to be worshiped as God (verse 4).

John paints the same portrait of the beast that Daniel unveils—bestial (verse 4), blatant (verse 5), blasphemous (verse 6), belligerent (verse 7). John concurs with Daniel that the ten kings will recognize the absolute authority of the dictator (Revelation 17:12,13). He anticipates the collapse of the empire of the beast (Revelation 16:10) and finally sees the beast seized and his armies destroyed in the lake of fire (Revelation 19:19,20). John, like Daniel (Daniel 7:12), even intimates that the destruction of the beast himself and his kingdom will not be the finale of end time events, for a remnant of armies will need to be dealt with and destroyed after the slaying of the beast and his armies (Revelation 19:21).

The Son of man will triumph over the man of sin.

FOOD FOR THOUGHT

"Power tends to corrupt; absolute power corrupts absolutely."

—Lord Acton

NOW TEST YOUR KNOWLEDGE

Match the following:

1. The great sea
2. The four winds
3. The Ancient of days
4. The Son of man
5. The ten horns
6. The little horn
7. The ministering thousands
8. The fourth beast
9. The everlasting kingdom
10. The saints of the most High

a. kings of the future
b. millennial reign
c. Christ the Son
d. universal commotion
e. Mediterranean
f. ten-state unity
g. God the Father
h. final beast-emperor
i. Jewish believers
j. angels

AUG 2, 1981

The Northern Destroyer

LESSON SCRIPTURE
Daniel 8

RELATED SCRIPTURE
Isaiah 20:1-6; 29:1-8; 36; 37; Ezekiel 38;
39; Matthew 24:15-22; Revelation 8; 9.

LESSON AIM
To leave matters in God's hands.

LEARN BY HEART
"So let all thine enemies perish, O Lord:
but let them that love him be as the sun
when he goeth forth in his might" (Judges
5:31).

EVERY DAY WITH THE WORD

**STUDENT'S
NOTEBOOK**

This column is for the
student who desires
additional study of
the lesson theme.

Monday	Victory over Pharoah	Exodus 14:13-31
Tuesday	Victory over Balaam	Numbers 23:1-12
Wednesday	Victory at Gibeon	Joshua 10:1-14
Thursday	Victory over Philistines	I Samuel 17:31-52
Friday	Victory over Assyria	II Kings 19:20-35
Saturday	Victory over Prince Rosh	Ezekiel 38
Sunday	Victory over the beast	Revelation 15

LESSON PREPARATION

Have you read or
heard about Middle
East confrontation
recently? How has
this affected your
interest in prophecy?

The eyes of the world are riveted on the Middle
East. Newscasters repeatedly declare that it is the
strategic center of the world. Almost daily, Arabs
and Jews exchange raids or at least hostile words.
Nations outside the Middle East are anything but
neutral. Everyone seems to agree that the Middle

East constitutes one of the most potentially explosive areas in the world.

The Middle East—this center of world attention—commands a center stage position in Daniel 8—12. Chapter 8 mentions Israel's sacrifices and sanctuary, her crime and chastening. Palestine will explode with invasion, and this chapter introduces us to it.

THE INGREDIENTS OF THE VISION (Daniel 8:1-14)

Daniel consistently gives the time, place, and circumstances of the divine revelations which came to him. The Biblical writers take special pains to link all events to calendar dates and geographic places. Time and history are thus connected to eternity. God intervenes in history; God acts in history. In the Scriptures we have a history of redemption and a history of the kingdom. The time of the vision is the third year of Belshazzar's regency; the place is Susa in Persia, not Babylon; and more specific than that, Daniel stands (in vision) on the banks of the Ulai, a river on which Susa was built (verses 1,2).

Daniel saw a ram standing on the side of the river, about to begin a westward assault in which it would crush every opponent in its path. The angel Gabriel interpreted the meaning (verse 20). The ram signifies the dual kingdom of the Medes and Persians. The shorter horn (verse 3) is a fit emblem of Media because the Medes did not continue in power after Darius. The longer horn which came up later pictures the ascendancy of the Persians over the Medes under the leadership of Cyrus.

Classical writers refer to the Ulai as the Eulaeus, an artificial canal which flowed near Susa on the north and northeast, connecting the Kerkha and Abdizful Rivers.

The "notable" horn (verse 5) is a "conspicuous" spike.

While Daniel was reflecting upon the ram, he saw a goat coming from the opposite direction and moving with great speed toward the East. The animal had a single horn protruding from its head, and with that fearful horn the goat charged into the ram in a blind fury, knocking the ram to the ground and tramping upon it. The goat became mighty in power; but at the zenith of its strength the horn was broken, and four other horns came up in its place.

Gabriel gave the meaning of these details, too (verse 21). The horn is the king of Greece. We know him as the famous son of Philip of Macedon—Alexander the Great. The Persians had invaded Greek territories and had infuriated the Greeks by their treacherous and bloodthirsty deeds. With the newly devised army Alexander cut to pieces the Persians and with phenomenal success expanded his empire until it reached India. It is reported that Alexander wept because no territories were left to be conquered.

In less than 13 years Alexander conquered the world of his time.

Alexander died at the age of 33 of a condition brought about by a dissolute life. He simply did not have the resistance to throw off a tropical fever. He had no heir, and so his four generals divided the vast empire between themselves. This is the meaning of the four horns (verse 8).

Remember one important rule of interpreting prophecy: similarity is not necessarily identity. Learn to distinguish things that differ.

It is easy to follow the majority of Bible expositors and think that the little horn of Daniel 8 is identical to the little horn of Daniel 7. But this is a hasty conclusion. Many students of prophecy (especially American writers) believe that chapter 8 is a clarification of chapter 7 and that chapter 8 pinpoints the geographic area from which the antichrist will come. They are confusing three separate and distinct end-time leaders and making prophecy even more complicated than it already is. Careful study will show that neither the little horn of chapter 7 nor the little horn of chapter 8 is the antichrist; and the little horn of chapter 7 is an entirely different person from the little horn of chapter 8. About the only similarity between them is that both persecute Israel, but this is not enough to equate them.

The little horn of Daniel 8 had his initial historical fulfillment in the person and performances of Antiochus Epiphanes (175-164 B.C.). Antiochus had his origin in the northern section of Alexander's divided empire. Antiochus swept down from the North and inflicted terrible atrocities upon the Jews. He marched his armies through Palestine to Egypt. His northern connections, his Egyptian campaign, and his destruction of the land of Palestine make him the ancient predecessor of the coming king of the North, *not* of the emperor-beast in Europe.

The noncanonical book of Maccabees describes Antiochus' tyranny. It is not Scripture, but the histories are quite reliable. Josephus also relates some of these events.

Daniel described Antiochus' activities in verses 10-14, and in many of these details Antiochus resembles the future Assyrian whom God will use to chastise Israel. Antiochus elevated himself to the stars of heaven and magnified himself as the equal of any god (verses 10,11). The Assryian of old boasted in his own strength (Isaiah 10:13), magnifying himself above all others (verse 15).

"The transgression" plays a prominent part in Antiochus' activities (Daniel 8:12,13,23). Likewise, God will employ the services of the Assyrian to punish Israel for "the transgression," which represents a return to idolatry. The armies of the Assyrian Sennacherib were used by God to chasten Israel for idolatry, and God will raise up a successor to the Assyrian in the future who will

God sent Antiochus to punish the Jews because of their sin (Daniel 8:12).

Scriptures about the
Assyrian: Isaiah
10:24,25; 14:24-27;
30:31-33; Joel 2;
Micah 5:1-6; 7:12.

punish Israel for entering into an alliance with the Western allies—a treaty held together by the erection of an idol in the Jewish temple. God will use the Assyrian of the future to disannul the diabolical compact (Isaiah 28:14-18).

"Desolation" is associated with Antiochus (Daniel 8:13), and it is the northern invader of the end-time whom God will use to devastate Israel's land. "The abomination of desolation" refers to the ruination that the northern invasion will cause in Palestine on account of the idolatrous connection between Israel and the kingdom of the beast of Europe. Daniel 9:27 speaks of the "desolate"— that is the "desolator," and we shall study it in the next lesson. Joel 2 describes the desolation which the northern army will bring to Palestine.

The present return of Israel to the land and the marvelous restoration of the land is prepatory to the destruction that the nation shall experience when the armies of the North reduce it to waste and ruin.

Antiochus will tread the people under his feet (verse 13). Again, this is the same language that is used of the Assyrian in Isaiah 28:18, where God warns the Jews that they will be trodden down by the overflowing scourge of the northern army. A careful study of all the passages that pertain to the king of the North and to the Assyrian will show that Antiochus is more akin to him than to the western dictator.

THE INTERPRETATION OF THE VISION
(Daniel 8:15-27)

Daniel 8 is perfectly clear about the ultimate fulfillment of the prophecy about the little horn. It will be consummated in a period just short of three and one half years (verse 14), at a time when the Jewish temple has been rebuilt and the Mosaic ritual restored, at a time of God's indignation—in short, at the time of the end (verses 17,19) and in

Daniel 8:14 reads
literally "2300
evenings and

the latter time of Israel's transgression (verse 23).

Nothing can be more certain than that Antiochus did not totally fulfill the content of these prophecies. A double fulfillment is in view here—a fulfillment to occur at the end of the times of the Gentiles, as well as fulfillment in Antiochus' time. "The time of the end" marks the period immediately before Christ returns to set up the kingdom of David. It is the period of the seven-year tribulation, sometimes called "Daniel's seventieth week." The time of the end is appointed (verse 19)—that is, fixed in the eternal counsels. And that time is especially designed by God to complete His whole work in Israel before bringing the nation into the era of Messiah's earthly reign.

The moment the image of the beast is erected in the temple, God will bring the northern king of fierce countenance against the land of Israel (verse 23). Daniel begins his description of the invader in verses 23-25 and continues it in chapter 11, verses 40-45. The "fierce countenance" implies his impudence and shameless disregard for God and man. He is unmoving in his feelings and pursues a cruel course without reluctance. "Understanding dark sentences" means that he knows how to use falsehood and dissimulation. He says one thing and means another. He phrases his words in such a way as to deceive. In his own right he is powerful enough, but in addition to that, he is supported by another government (Daniel 8:24). The king of the North is a confederate of Prince Rosh (Ezekiel 38:2,4-6). The armies of the extreme North combine with the king of the North and other countries to invade Palestine. The results of the invasion are devastating; many Jews

mornings." Verses 11-14 are talking about discontinuation of 2300 evening and morning sacrifices. It requires 1150 days to offer that many sacrifices—3½ years on the Jewish calendar.

Deuteronomy 28:50; Isaiah 19:4

"Dark sentences" may imply that the king of the North depends upon occult powers; he is in league with the devil. The double-talk sounds like what the Western world has heard from Russia for decades.

suffer death. Others escape the area before the invasion and flee to the mountains in obedience to the instructions of Jesus in Matthew 24:15-22. Others make their perilous journey through Jordan to the rose red city of Petra (Isaiah 16:1-4). But these details belong to the other prophets; space and time forbid a study of all these events now.

The king of the North will make the Jews think that they are safe, and while they are saying, "peace and safety," sudden destruction will come upon them from the North. The peace mentioned in Daniel 8:25 is probably equivalent to the era of peace that will immediately follow the rapture of the church (Revelation 6:2-4). Ezekiel gives the same conditions. He puts the invasion of Prince Rosh and all his confederate armies at a time when the Jews think they are perfectly secure (Ezekiel 38:8,11,14). Israel is not really safe; she only imagines it. She is depending upon the western dictator to defend her, and she has been listening to the "dark sentences" of the king of the North who has deceived her into trusting him. It may even be that the arms race has been halted, each side pledging to reduce its warheads.

But the northern aggressor goes too far (Daniel 8:25); he contests the authority of the Messiah and meets his doom by a supernatural intervention of God. "Broken without hand" indicates that no human hand or army will defeat the king of the North and the Russian armies backing him. The prophets and John the revelator concur in their explanation of this destruction. The ground will literally open and swallow up the king of the North and the Russians. Joel informs us that some will escape to the desert region where they will

He will take advantage of the Jews being in a state of ease and unprepared for wily encroachments.

69

perish in the burning sands. Ezekiel suggests that a sixth of the army will return to its place in the North.

The future Assyrian, king of the North and successor to Antiochus, is prominent on the prophetic page; in fact, much more space is given to him than to the emperor-beast in Europe or to the Jewish antichrist in Palestine.

FOOD FOR THOUGHT

"God requires no mighty instrument to cast down a tyrant. He can adopt the most insignificant means to that end."

—Starke

Choose the correct answers:

1. Daniel 8—12 was written in (a) Greek; (b) Aramaic; (c) Hebrew.
2. Daniel's vision was interpreted by (a) Michael; (b) Abednego; (c) Gabriel.
3. The ram signified (a) Babylon; (b) Medo-Persia; (c) Greece.
4. The goat signified (a) Greece; (b) Rome; (c) Russia.
5. The notable horn referred to (a) Pontius Pilate; (b) Alexander the Great; (c) Antiochus.
6. The four horns depict (a) four of the ten kings of the future; (b) archangels; (c) Alexander's four generals.
7. The little horn represents the predecessor of the future (a) Assyrian (king of the North); (b) beast of Europe; (c) Prince Rosh.
8. The "transgression" of Israel is (a) lack of repentance; (b) idolatry; (c) compromise.
9. The king of the North will be backed by (a) the Russians; (b) the Jews; (c) the Egyptians.

God's Timetable For Israel

LESSON SCRIPTURE
Daniel 9

RELATED SCRIPTURE
Isaiah 53; Hosea 5:5—6:2; Zechariah 13:1-9; Matthew 21:33-46; 23:34-39; John 10:1-13.

LESSON AIM
To seek to know God's will through prayer and Bible study.

LEARN BY HEART
"To the Lord our God belong mercies and forgivenesses, though we have rebelled against him" (Daniel 9:9).

9

EVERY DAY WITH THE WORD

Monday	Reliance on God	Psalm 17
Tuesday	Answered prayer	Psalm 28
Wednesday	God's forgiveness	Psalm 51
Thursday	God's favor	Psalm 80
Friday	God's faithfulness	Psalm 89:20-37
Saturday	Israel's unfaithfulness	Psalm 106:1-40
Sunday	Israel's regathering	Psalm 147

STUDENT'S NOTEBOOK

This column is for the student who desires additional study of the lesson theme.

LESSON PREPARATION

How can the people of our generation go about their daily routine completely indifferent to the trends and perils of our time? Why do our diplomats sit in solemn council vainly trying to bring about national and international peace? Why do presidential candidates promise a new and glorious era ahead for democracy?

As sincere as their intentions may be, they nevertheless reach false conclusions and indulge in misplaced optimism because they are not students of the prophetic Scriptures. Therefore, they cannot see that history is running in the mold of prophecy and that it is moving in the direction of totalitarianism and turmoil.

Daniel 9 illustrates the fact that human history is the outworking of a divine program for Israel. The events of the calendar all contribute in some way to God's purposes for them.

THE PRAYERFUL CONFESSION
(Daniel 9:1-19)

A study of the prophetic Word inscribed by the pen of Jeremiah motivated Daniel to prayer and penitence. He was turned to sorrow by what he learned about the future of his erring people. The time of the events of Daniel 9 occurred in "the first year of Darius" (verse 1). Darius is identified as the son of Ahasuerus (Artaxerxes I), racially a Mede and royally a king whom Cyrus appointed to manage the affairs of Babylon.

Sometime during Darius' first year of rule (between 538 and 537 B.C.) Daniel was studying the prophecies of Jeremiah 25:11,12; 29:10. He was a prophet himself but he was not above a diligent investigation of the written Word. Furthermore, he had no objection to studying the writings of another prophet (verse 2). Daniel learned from Jeremiah that the captivity would last for 70 years. The Jews had not observed the 7th year Sabbath

The only safe place to cast an anchor is in Christ. He will never disappoint our hopes (I Peter 2:6).

The Apostle Paul felt the same intense sorrow for the unbelieving nation (Romans 9:2,3; 10:1).

No one outgrows his need of daily study of the Word of God.

rest for 70 years, and so God sent them into exile and caused the land to lie desolate for the equivalent number of those unobserved Sabbath years.

II Chronicles 36:21

The knowledge that only a few months remained before the fulfillment of the prophecy struck Daniel with mingled grief and gladness. The Jews in captivity were in no condition of heart to receive the fulfillment of the promise. Unbelieving and disobedient people can never expect the blessing of divine promises and provisions. Daniel set himself to a prayer of adoration, confession, intercession, and petition (verses 3-19), for he knew this was a condition that had to be met before God would return the people from the land of their exile.

Jeremiah 29:12

The prayer is a perfect model, for it begins with a recognition of God's person and power. Daniel worshiped the great and awesome God. He continued with testimonies to God's character: God is faithful not to break His covenant with Israel; He is the merciful God (verse 4). Daniel then spread the sins of the nation, including himself, before the Lord. They had run the gamut—iniquity, wickedness, rebellion, departure, and defection (verse 5). They had neither heeded nor harkened to God's servants, the prophets, who repeatedly tried to recall them to repentance (verse 6). Daniel vindicated God for what followed Israel's sin (verses 7-14). They deserved all the confusion, calamity, and curses which had come upon them. God had carried out His threat against the nation in faithfulness to His Word.

Study Psalm 89 for information about the inviolate nature of the covenants. The nation will be punished for its sins, but God will not revoke or invalidate His promises.

It is significant that Daniel refers to the Mosaic covenant rather than to the Abrahamic covenant (verses 11,13). The people had broken the conditional Mosaic law, but Daniel did not believe for a single moment that as a consequence the nation had forfeited forever the promise that it would rule for God as a kingdom of priests. Daniel was still looking for a fulfillment of theocratic blessings on the basis of the Mosaic, Palestinian, and Davidic covenants.

The book of Hosea best illustrates this principle of breach. There it is a breach of the marriage vows. Nevertheless, God will restore the faithless wife out of the riches of His great mercy.

The fulfillment of the covenants does not depend ultimately upon Israel's faithfulness but upon God's faithfulness. Israel did not deserve anything from God. The nation was responsible for a breach of covenant and earned forfeiture of all the glorious privileges of kingship over the nations, but Daniel pled God's forgiveness and mercy (verses 9,18,19). Daniel's prayer is a foreshadowing of the repentance and prayer of the nation at the end of the tribulation when the people will mourn over their sin and call upon their long-rejected Messiah to come and save them (Zechariah 12:10). Of course, God cannot fulfill the provisions of His covenant promises while they continue in their sins, but the tribulation judgments are designed by God to bring the nation to its knees, and this is precisely what will happen.

THE PROPHETIC CALENDAR
(Daniel 9:20-27)

Daniel had his devotions regularly. Do you?

Daniel's prayer moved Heaven to immediate response. Gabriel was dispatched with information about the nation's future. Flying swiftly, he reached the praying prophet at the time when the evening oblation was formerly offered at Jerusalem. For nearly 70 years the Mosaic rites had been discontinued, but Daniel evidently observed the morning and evening offerings in the only way he could—in prayer facing the beloved city.

With an admonition to Daniel to consider the vision, the angel began to unfold a chronology of events that pertained exclusively to Daniel's people and Daniel's holy city (verse 24).

Daniel 9:24-27 gives a schedule of a segment of Israel's national history during which God will carry out the six purposes of verse 24. The history is restricted to 70 seven-year periods or 490 years. This period has a specific point of beginning and ending. It commences with the decree of Artaxerxes to rebuild the city of Jerusalem. The earlier edicts of Cyrus, Darius, and Artaxerxes do not qualify as a starting point for this 490 year history because none of them related to the city; they only provided for the rebuilding of the temple.

The decree was issued in 445 B.C. See Nehemiah 2:3,5,8.

Earlier edicts are spoken of in II Chronicles 36:22,23; Ezra 1:1-4; 6:1-5,8-12; 7:11-26.

The 490 years are divided into three segments, and the angel indicates what activities will transpire during these three parts. During the first 7 weeks (49 years) the city with its streets and walls will be rebuilt; then 62 weeks (434 years) will be added to the 7 weeks before the Messiah arrives. From the commandment to Christ the King, then, a total of 483 years will expire. The termination of these 483 years came on the day of the triumphal entry in March-April, A.D. 30, when Jesus Christ, for the first and only time, presented Himself officially as Israel's Prince and Messianiac King.

At the end of the 69 weeks (483 years) the Messiah is "cut off" (Daniel 9:26). Instead of entering into the era of His kingly reign, He receives nothing. Israel rejected His regal claims to the throne of David and sentenced Him to a crimi-

Israel in the decision of her national representatives finally and officially rejected Him at the time of the triumphal entry. From that point on the kingdom was deferred until that day when the nation officially welcomes Him back (Hosea 5:15; Matthew 23:39).

nal's death. The six divine purposes which God intends to accomplish in the nation in the course of the 490-year period were deferred to the last week (7 years). Between the 69th and the 70th week we have an indeterminate period, during which Jerusalem suffers from a flood of invaders. The 70th week did not follow the 69th week successively. "The" transgression has not been finished; in fact, Israel's final apostasy is still ahead. God has not made an end of the nation's sins; the people are yet nationally blinded and continue in their unbelief. The nation has not entered into the provisions of reconciliation; neither has it experienced a practical righteousness. The prophecies regarding the nation have not been fulfilled, and the temple has not been anointed at the end of the 69 weeks.

All of these promises will be fulfilled to Israel during the course of the 70th week (the 7-year period of the tribulation). During the long interval between the 69th and 70th week Jerusalem was destroyed by Titus (in A.D. 70), and this destruction has been followed by a continual succession of Gentile rulers who have trampled the city and the land under foot. This desolation will continue through the entire present church age and right on into the tribulation era.

Luke 21:20-24

Luke 21 traces the troubles from A.D. 70 to the end of the tribulation. Matthew 24 limits its subject to the troubles of the tribulation.

The angel told Daniel what would happen in the last 7 years of the seventy weeks. A Roman prince will appear who will guarantee Israel military protection from the "flood" of northern armies. A treaty will be ratified which pledges to Israel territorial sovereignty for 7 years (verse 27). It assures her of peace with her Arab neighbors. Israel will rebuild the temple and reintroduce the Mosaic sacrificial system. She will depend upon

77

her national representative and king—the Jewish antichrist—to secure her borders by his diplomatic relations with the Roman prince of Europe.

At the middle of the seven-year period the European beast-emperor will ban the Mosaic ordinances and instruct the Jewish antichrist to place an idol in the holy of holies. In order to get continued military protection, the apostate Jews will comply with the demand. Many saved Jews will refuse to worship the image and will not receive the mark of the beast. Their lives will stand in jeopardy. The erection of the image of the European beast is the signal for these saved Jews to flee the city, for on the heels of idolatry will come God's avenger—the northern destroyer.

"Overspreading" pertains to military protection. "Abominations" refers to idolatry. The word "desolate" should be rendered "desolator." God will respond to a new and unprecedented outbreak of idolatry in Israel by sending the king of the North into Palestine to chastise Israel. The northern armies (the Assyrian) will devastate the land until God has accomplished His purpose, and then the fearful desolator will meet his doom on the mountains of Israel by a divine judgment on the armies. During the northern assault the antichrist has apparently fled, and the European beast has failed to live up to his treaty obligations with Israel.

A moment's reflection on Isaiah 28:14-18 will help to clarify the situation that will prevail during the 70th week. This passage relates the boasting confidence of the people of Israel who will enter into a diabolical alliance with death and Hell (verse 15). They will place their hopes for political and religious security in lies and falsehood.

The Jews will be at ease in Zion (Amos 6:1). See I Thessalonians 5:3.

Matthew 24:15 presupposes that the temple will be rebuilt.

Matthew 24:15-22

Deuteronomy 7:25,26

Joel 2

Isaiah 14:24-27

Zechariah 11:17; John 10:13

II Thessalonians
2:9-12; Psalm 5:6;
Revelation 13:14

Revelation 16:13

They will listen to the lies of the false prophet—the antichrist. He will deceive them into thinking that they are safe. God calls the treaty a covenant with Hell because the European dictator and the Jewish deceiver are both energized by the devil.

The Jews imagine that these two fiends will protect them from the "overflowing scourge"—the northern desolator. Their confidence, however, is pinned on the wrong object. Military agreements with the west will not save them from the king of the North. The armies of the North will descend like a flood of waters, and God will use the desolator to annul the East-West alliance (Isaiah 28:18). At first the armies of the West will not retaliate. They will simply deliberate and call for a withdrawal of the troops (Ezekiel 38:13).

FOOD FOR THOUGHT

"Prayer is not overcoming God's reluctance; it is laying hold of His highest willingness."
—Richard Chenevix Trench

NOW TEST YOUR KNOWLEDGE

Answer true or false:

1. Daniel had been studying the prophecy of Amos.
2. Daniel appealed to God on the grounds of his own worthiness.
3. Daniel referred to the covenant with Moses.
4. Daniel's prayer was answered by Michael.
5. The prophecy pertained only to the Jews.
6. The 490 years commenced with the birth of Christ.
7. The 69th week concluded with the day of Pentecost.
8. Jerusalem was destroyed by Titus in A.D. 70.
9. The interval between the 69th and 70th weeks is 200 years long.
10. Israel will enter into an agreement with the beast of Europe.

The Invisible World of Spirits

10

LESSON SCRIPTURE
Daniel 10

RELATED SCRIPTURE
I Corinthians 6:2,3; Galatians 1:6-9;
Hebrews 1; I Peter 1:12; II Peter 2:4;
Revelation 4; 9

LESSON AIM
To have a personal time alone with God.

LEARN BY HEART
"But they that wait upon the Lord shall
renew their strength; they shall mount up
with wings as eagles; they shall run, and
not be weary; and they shall walk, and not
faint" (Isaiah 40:31).

EVERY DAY WITH THE WORD

**STUDENT'S
NOTEBOOK**

This column is for the
student who desires
additional study of
the lesson theme.

Monday	Interviewed by angels	Genesis 18:1-22
Tuesday	Fed by an angel	I Kings 19:1-7
Wednesday	Purged by an angel	Isaiah 6:1-8
Thursday	Served by angels	Matthew 4:1-11
Friday	Strengthened by an angel	Luke 22:39-46
Saturday	Rescued by an angel	Acts 12:1-17
Sunday	Visited by an angel	Hebrews 13:1-9

LESSON PREPARATION

Romans 5:6

Our mighty God rolls the planets in their orbits
around the sun and sustains with unwearied arms
the circuits of stellar space, but it is an infinitely
greater work for Him to lift up us poor, weak
creatures and replenish our sagging spirits. When
we were without strength, Christ died for us, and

now we can do all things through Him who makes us strong.

Philippians 4:13

Daniel knew what it was to be strengthened by God's might in his inner man. He had realized the truth of the promise found in Isaiah 40:29: "He giveth power to the faint; and to them that have no might he increaseth strength."

Ephesians 3:16

Psalm 27:1

THE EXPERIENCE OF DANIEL
(Daniel 10:1-9)

The Holy Spirit who moved Daniel to record his experiences must have wanted to convey to us the value of definiteness, for Daniel invariably began with dates, names, and places (Daniel 10:1). The name "Belteshazzar" accompanied the name "Daniel" as if to give further identity to the man. This is the very same Daniel who was taken captive as a youth, brought to Nebuchadnezzar's court, and given a pagan name years earlier. He had continued his administrative work until the first year of Cyrus' reign (Daniel 1:21) and now in semi-retirement in the third year of Cyrus (535 B.C.), Daniel could say with the Apostle Paul, "Having therefore obtained help of God, I continue unto this day, witnessing both to small and great" (Acts 26:22).

Are you this definite about the time and place of your fellowship with God?

Daniel had been overcome with grief and gave himself to mourning for three weeks (Daniel 10:2). More than two years had passed since Cyrus had issued (in 538 B.C.) the command which permitted the Jews to return to Jerusalem. You would think that Daniel would have been singing the 126th Psalm. Why was not his mouth filled with laughter and his tongue with singing?

II Chronicles 36:22, 23; Ezra 1:1-3

Why was he not shouting, "The Lord hath done great things for us; whereof we are glad"?

The sorrows of the prophet derived from his knowledge that only a relatively small number of Jews (49,897) had returned to the homeland. The great majority, including princes and priests, had preferred their comfortable homes and positions in Babylon's beautiful environs to the desolation of Palestine and the hardships that awaited them there. Daniel had heard that those who were in Jerusalem had met with the opposition of the Samaritans. Some of the people had fallen into indifference, and others were depressed and discouraged. The feeble remnant had actually ceased their labors on the temple, and these facts were enough to bring Daniel to his knees. The aged prime minister took no interest in food, wine, or anointing (Daniel 10:3). He could not interrupt his intercession before God long enough to refresh his languishing body.

But gloom was transformed to glory by the appearing of "a certain man clothed in linen" (verse 5). Debate continues about the identity of the heavenly visitor. But the sevenfold similarity between the description in verses 5,6 and the description in Revelation 1:13-16 is rather convincing evidence that Daniel was face to face with a Christophany—an appearance of Christ in His preincarnate form.

The linen speaks of Christ's perfect righteousness, His absolutely sinless humanity. The golden girdle is an emblem of His deity and glory. It signifies His permanence, preciousness, and purity. The word "girded" denotes His sovereignty and strength.

His body was like beryl (Daniel 10:6). No one

Ezra 2:64,65

Read the accounts of Jewish problems in Ezra 4:1-5,12-22.

The most helpful exposition of Daniel 10:5,6 is to be found in M. L. Lowe's book, Christ in the Book of Daniel, chapter 7. You will be greatly enriched by this beautiful treatment.

is certain about the meaning of many of the gems of the Bible, but beryl is probably either a yellow topaz or a blue-green stone like the emerald. If the topaz is meant, it suggests His glory. If the emerald is in view, it intimates His grace. The lightning recalls the dazzling brilliance and suddenness of His arrival. Lightning is the precursor to a storm, and here it may speak of the approaching judgment. His eyes were like lamps of fire. This depicts His omniscience and severity. Like burning X rays, His eyes can penetrate to the very marrow of the bones. His feet were like the color of brass—another emblem of judgment. The voice like thunder refers to His omnipotence and authority. The dead will hear the voice of omnipotence and rise from their graves.

Matthew 24:27

Brass or bronze indicates judgment. See Numbers 21:8,9.

John 5:28,29; 11:43; I Thessalonians 4:16.

The reaction of Daniel to the vision corresponds to John's reaction in Revelation 1:17 and to Paul's response in Acts 9:4. Only Daniel actually saw the Lord and heard His words. His companions probably were dazzled by the light and deafened by the thunderous tones. They fled from the scene in terror (Daniel 10:7). Paul's companions had much the same experience on the Damascus Road (Acts 9:7).

Daniel was left alone in the divine presence (Daniel 10:8). He had an experience similar to that of Moses, who was covered with the glory of the Lord upon Mount Sinai. Moses reported that "the sight of the glory of the Lord was like devouring fire" (Exodus 24:17). The presence of God in His holiness had the same effect upon Daniel that it had upon Isaiah, who sensed his own leprous corruption (Isaiah 6:5). Like Ezekiel, Daniel collapsed on the ground (Daniel 10:9; see Ezekiel 1:28). Nothing but an appearance of Deity

Study the following men in their solitude with God: Abraham (Genesis 13); Jacob (Genesis 32:24); Moses (Exodus 3:1); Elijah (I Kings 17:1-7); Paul (Galatians 1:17).

can account for Daniel's prostration in Daniel 10:8,9.

THE EXERCISES OF ANGELS
(Daniel 10:10-21)

For the second time Daniel felt an angelic touch (verse 10; see 8:18). The Lord of glory is not the subject of verses 10-14; instead, Gabriel—a subordinate and servant of the Lord—ministered to Daniel, helped him to a crouching position, assured him of the divine favor, and encouraged him to get to his feet (verse 11).

The trembling Daniel listened while Gabriel explained the reason for the delayed answer to his prayer (verses 12,13). The angel had begun his journey to earth 21 days earlier when Daniel had first abandoned himself to grief and prayer, but the angel was intercepted en route by the prince of Persia, and was able to continue his flight earthward only after the archangel Michael had come to his defense and released him from the clutches of the adversary.

Here the veil between the physical and spiritual world is lifted momentarily. Only on rare occasions does the Scripture take us behind the scenes of world events to the invisible world of spirits. Jacob saw angels ascending and descending on the ladder staircase to Heaven (Genesis 28:12). On his return from Haran, Jacob was met by "God's host"—angelic guardians (Genesis 32:1,2). Elisha's servant saw the heavenly warriors hovering over the impending battle at Dothan (II Kings 6:17). Jesus gave us a glimpse of the unseen world in Luke 16 where He described the conditions of the wicked and the righ-

Note the contrast between the answer to the prayer in the 9th chapter. On that occasion Daniel didn't have time to finish his prayer before the response came. You can make a profitable study on answers to prayer by consulting the subject in Nave's Topical Bible.

teous after their death. Jesus promised that the authorities of the invisible realm would never overthrow the church (Matthew 16:18). He did not correct the devil's boast that he had the power to give Jesus the kingdoms of the world (Matthew 4:8,9).

The Apostle Paul reminded the churches that Satan is the prince of the power of the air. The airways above earth seem to be the special theater of his activity. Christ in His ascent through the air after His resurrection encountered principalities and powers which He defeated victoriously (Colossians 2:15). Believers are called upon to wrestle with these principalities and powers "in high places" (Ephesians 6:12). "The weapons of our warfare are not carnal, but mighty through God to the pulling down of strong holds" (II Corinthians 10:4).

The Word of God gives us every reason to think that demonic intelligences govern world powers behind the scenes. Paul calls them "rulers of the darkness of this world" (Ephesians 6:12)—literally, "world-rulers of this darkness." Daniel 10 is the first reference to the fact that the empires of earth are influenced by satanic personalities in the demon world. Human government is subject to demon manipulation. Satan has assigned certain fallen angels to political activities among the nations in order that Satan's program can be carried out in an organized and systematic way. The devil is not omnipotent or omnipresent; therefore, he has to depend upon agents who are accountable to him.

We are given to understand also that the holy angels act on behalf of the affairs of men and nations. Michael, particularly, is the guardian and

The writer of Hebrews makes a special point of calling the reader's attention to the fact that Christ passed through the heavens (Hebrews 4:14) as if to suggest the hostile territory through which He must pass. Christ will come into the air rather than to allow the church to traverse the devil's territory alone (I Thessalonians 4:17).

protector of Israel. He is responsible for preserving the people through generations of dispersion and persecution. Michael and his angels are engaged in an unremitting war—a war to be climaxed in the tribulation—against the devil and his angels (Revelation 12:7). Michael engaged in a dispute with the devil over the body of Moses (Jude 9). An angel will lay hold of Satan and cast him into the abyss for 1000 years (Revelation 20:1-3).

"Tutelary" pertains to the exercise of authority and guardianship.

Gabriel expected another assault from the tutelary demon prince of Persia on his heavenward flight. He intimated also that the time would come when he would fight with a principality who was responsible to influence the Greek government (Daniel 10:20). Everything points to the fact that each nation is directed in its evil purposes by a mastermind—Satan—who appoints demon princes over the world system.

As soon as the Greek empire would come on the scene, it too would be influenced by demon power.

The whole effect of the information and the angelic speech combined to stupefy and strip Daniel of his strength (verses 15,16). The identity of the being in verses 16,17 has not been settled to everyone's satisfaction. At any rate, Gabriel is evidently in view in verses 18,19 because he touches Daniel and addresses him as the "man greatly beloved" as he did before (see verses 10,11).

The work of calming, consoling and caring for God's people is certainly the work of angels. Both Jesus and Daniel knew the keeping power of angels (Psalm 91:11,12). The angels are chiefly characterized by wisdom and strength. Their special ministry to the saints is to assure their physical safety and well-being. Angels calm men's fears (Luke 1:30) and stand by their side to strengthen and cheer them (Acts 27:23,24). Nothing in Daniel 10:18,19 is incompatible with what we read elsewhere in Scripture about the duties of angels.

The final word of Gabriel to Daniel was that he had come to show Daniel "that which is noted in the scripture of truth" (verse 21). The events that will come to pass are already written in the decrees of God and therefore are sure and final. The course of events cannot be altered.

God is able to bring everything to pass just as He plans. He is all-knowing and all-powerful. Isn't it comforting to have the sovereign God for your heavenly Father?

Daniel was thus strengthened to receive the forthcoming details of end-time events—matters which concerned his own people in the latter days (verse 14). The last two chapters of the book unfold these momentous events.

FOOD FOR THOUGHT

"The devil is worthy of some honor; he minds his business and is wide awake in this sleepy, drowsy age."

—Anonymous

Match the following:

1. Daniel grieved because only a small remnant had returned to _____.
2. _____ had a similar experience to Daniel's in that he saw Jehovah.
3. The "prince of Persia" refers to _____.
4. Demons perform their duties in _____.
5. Christians are in a _____ with demons.
6. _____ is Israel's guardian angel.
7. Gabriel called Daniel _____.
8. The answer to Daniel's prayer was _____.
9. Christ's feet were colored like brass, signifying _____.
10. Christ's righteousness was shown by his _____ clothing.

a. love
b. Michael
c. speeded
d. Nehemiah
e. judgment
f. Jerusalem
g. linen
h. Moses
i. a demon
j. Cyrus
k. delayed
l. "blessed"
m. the earth
n. "man greatly beloved"
o. battle

Invasions Sweep the Middle East

11

LESSON SCRIPTURE
Daniel 11:1-35

RELATED SCRIPTURE
Ezra 4—7; Nehemiah 2:1-10; Esther 1; 2;
Zechariah 9:1-8

LESSON AIM
To have faith that God will fulfill His Word
concerning future events.

LEARN BY HEART
"When the enemy shall come in like a
flood, the Spirit of the Lord shall lift up a
standard against him" (Isaiah 59:19).

EVERY DAY WITH THE WORD

Monday	Deceit and destruction	Psalm 35:1-20
Tuesday	The defiled temple	Psalm 79
Wednesday	Threats from the north	Psalm 80
Thursday	The day of trouble	Psalm 81
Friday	The enemies' plots	Psalm 83
Saturday	In angels' hands	Psalm 91
Sunday	Allied with God	Psalm 118:1-20

STUDENT'S NOTEBOOK

This column is for the student who desires additional study of the lesson theme.

LESSON PREPARATION

Mastery of the Scriptures forces the man of God to become a student of many other disciplines, especially of ancient history. There is no special merit in being able to recite the succession of Jewish, Persian, Greek, or Syrian kings. Nevertheless, God never condemns the acquisition of true knowledge. It should comfort no one

It is amazing how a study of the Bible involves geology, archaeology, astronomy, Hebrew and Greek, biology, psychology, philosophy, geography, and history. God's Word opens up new horizons in all the disciplines of knowledge.

that he is ignorant of the facts of history and has a narrow range of interests both secular and sacred. Daniel 11 is a taxing exercise in ancient history. It is God's Word and His story; therefore, it is worthy of our examination.

TWO CENTURIES OF INVASION
(Daniel 11:1-20)

The angel Gabriel first outlined the immediate successors to Cyrus (Daniel 11:2). The book of Ezra identifies them as Ahasuerus, Artaxerxes, and Darius. Secular historians call them Cambyses, Pseudo-Smerdis, and Darius Hystaspes respectively. They were followed by Xerxes, a king of vast resources who raided Greece in 480 B.C.

Cambyses, 529-522 B.C.; Smerdis, 522-521 B.C.; Darius, 521-485 B.C.; Xerxes, 486-465 B.C., was Ahasuerus of the book of Esther.

A lapse of time occurs between verses 3 and 4. The Spirit of God is silent about the successors to Xerxes because they have no bearing on the condition of the Jews. The mighty king of verse 3 was Alexander the Great, whose sprawling empire was divided at his death among his four generals because he had no heir (verse 4). The kingdom of Greece gradually wasted away and was finally "plucked up" by the Romans in 31 B.C.

Alexander, 336-323 B.C.

Verses 5-20 focus the spotlight upon the northern and the southern divisions of Alexander's territories. The king of the South represents the several Ptolemies of Egypt. The king of the North refers to the many rulers of Syria. The passage presents an amazing and detailed summary of the campaigns which Syria and Egypt waged against each other. In the military invasions northward and southward, Palestine usually became the battlefield of the warring factions and suffered the brunt of their revenge.

The prince of verse 5 was Alexander's Syrian general Seleucus I Nicator, who found it necessary to accept asylum in Egypt when Antigonas—an early Phrygian contender for Alexander's empire—routed him from the North. The king of the South was Ptolemy Lagus. With Ptolemy's help, Seleucus regained his authority and subsequently increased his dominions until his territories exceeded Ptolemy's.

Several years later an attempt was made to cement alliances between Egypt and Syria. Ptolemy Philadelphus of Egypt prevailed upon Antiochus II of Syria to marry his daughter Berenice. Antiochus put away his own wife Laodice and pronounced her children illegitmate. When Philadelphus died, Antiochus II took Laodice back, and she promptly murdered Berenice and her children. Later she poisoned her husband and put her son Callinicus on the throne of Syria. The marriage alliance proved an utter failure (verse 6).

Berenice's brother, Ptolemy III Euergetes, then invaded Syria in order to avenge his sister's death. He captured Antioch without opposition. Civil disorder erupted in Egypt, and Euergetes hastened home with a tremendous plunder (verses 7-9).

The sons of Callinicus wanted revenge against the attack of Euergetes. The first son, Ceraunus, reigned only two years. He was succeeded by his brother Antiochus III the Great. Antiochus III and his armies poured out of the North like a flood and deluged Palestine (verse 10). By this time Ptolemy Philopator had come to the Egyptian throne, and he repelled the northern invader at the battle of Raphia in 217 B.C. (verse 11). His military successes went to his head. He failed to follow through with his victory; consequently, Syria and

Seleucus served as admiral of Ptolemy's fleet.

The city of Laodicea was named after Laodice.

Ptolemy Philadelphus, according to tradition, brought 70 Jewish scholars to Egypt to prepare the Septuagint version (a Greek translation of the Hebrew Old Testament).

Egypt settled down to a kind of cold war for 13 years (verse 12).

Antiochus III the Great launched another campaign as soon as Philopator died. He managed to build an even larger army than he had before (verse 13). Antiochus secured the assistance of King Philip of Macedon and of the apostate Jews in Palestine who were glad to get free of Egyptian control (verse 14).

Antiochus was frustrated in his plan to conquer Egypt by the interference of Rome. He thereupon decided to take diplomatic measures by giving his daughter Cleopatra to Ptolemy Epiphanes, heir apparent to the Egyptian throne. Antiochus depended upon Cleopatra's allegiance. The tables were turned when Cleopatra repudiated her father and supported her husband (verse 17). Antiochus the Great then contented himself with plundering the coastlines and islands of the Mediterranean until Rome drove him out of Greece and later defeated him at Magnesia in 190 B.C. (verses 18,19). Antiochus' son, Seleucus Philopator, had to increase the tribute money which Rome exacted of his father. He was poisoned shortly after he sent Heliodorus his treasurer to pilfer the temple treasures at Jerusalem (verse 20).

The Sanhedrin welcomed Antiochus when he entered Jerusalem.

Antiochus reigned between 223-187 B.C.

Antiochus had to pay the highest indemnity known to antiquity—15,000 talents.

TEN YEARS OF INTRIGUE
(Daniel 11:21-35)

The kingdom really belonged to Demetrius, Antiochus IV's nephew. Antiochus IV pretended to be Demetrius' friend

Obtaining the help of King Eumenes II of Pergamum, Antiochus IV Epiphanes, the younger son of Antiochus III the Great, put down the legitimate heir to the Syrian throne and took the status of king. ''Vile'' is an appropriate epithet for this devilish man. Some of his subjects called him "Epimanes" meaning "Madman." He early won the affections of the people by his democratic ways, by the liberality which he displayed in the cities of Syria, by "his capricious fits of generosity," and by his able administration (Daniel 11:21-24).

When Antiochus heard that the Egyptian forces were preparing to invade Coele Syria, he forestalled them by crossing the frontier in 169 B.C. and drove them to Pelusium. He continued to Memphis where he concluded a treaty with Ptolemy Philometor. He had every intention of establishing an overlordship at Alexandria, but the people of Alexandria would not tolerate it. They repudiated Philometor and proclaimed his younger brother, Ptolemy Euergetes (usually called Physcon—"pot belly") as king (verse 26).

Antiochus was obliged by the lateness of the season to withdraw his troops. His operations had cost him enormously. He had to raise revenue, and so en route to Syria he sacked the temple at Jerusalem.

In 168 B.C. Antiochus pushed his forces against Egypt again, but Ptolemy Philometor and Physcon had solved their differences by this time and reigned jointly with Cleopatra (verse 27). Antiochus ravaged the Egyptian temples and sent his troops to beseige Alexandria, hoping that Rome would be too busy in Macedonia to take much notice. About a week before, however, Rome had concluded the Macedonian war with tremendous victory. The Roman senate sent Lucius Popillius Laenas with an ultimatum to Antiochus to leave Egypt alone. Antiochus reluctantly bowed to Rome and was frustrated in his

and took the regency while his nephew was hostage in Rome.

Alexander the Great founded Alexandria in 322 B.C. It became a great center of culture and one of the three largest cities in the Roman empire.

Antiochus wanted time to consult his advisors, but Laenas

drew a ring around him and warned him not to step out of it.

endeavor to conquer Egypt the second time (verse 30a).

The Jews in Palestine had to suffer the brunt of his wrath. He outlawed the Jewish ritual, the Sabbath observances, the dietary laws, and the rite of circumcision (verse 30b). He erected a new altar in honor of Zeus and burned offerings of swine flesh upon it. What followed was a thorough-going campaign of persecution, for the pious Jews refused to submit to Antiochus regardless of the penalties he imposed upon them for resistance (verse 31).

Chief among the resistance were a priest called Mattathias and his sons. They were strong and did exploits (verse 32). Insurgents gathered around Mattathias who demolished pagan altars, killed apostate Jews, and circumcised boys whose parents had feared to carry out the Mosaic legislation. Verse 33 summarizes in general the results of Jewish defiance during Antiochus' time and in the centuries which followed.

FOOD FOR THOUGHT

"What are all histories but God manifesting himself, shaking down and trampling under foot whatever he hath not planted."
—Oliver Cromwell

NOW TEST YOUR KNOWLEDGE

Match the following:

1. The last Persian king important to Jewish history.
2. Alexander's Syrian general.
3. The woman who reigned jointly with the Ptolemies.
4. The Egyptian king who avenged his sister's death.
5. The Syrian king who was assisted by Philip of Macedon.
6. The woman who poisoned Antiochus II.
7. The sister of Ptolemy III Euergetes.
8. The Roman ambassador who delivered a message to Antiochus Epiphanes.

a. Antiochus the Great
b. Berenice
c. Cleopatra
d. Popillius Laenas
e. Laodice
f. Ptolemy III Euergetes
g. Seleucus Nicator
h. Xerxes

Antichrist Faces an Emergency

12

LESSON SCRIPTURE
Daniel 11:36-45

RELATED SCRIPTURE
Genesis 4:1-17; Psalm 5; 7:11-17; Isaiah 30:1-14; 31; Jeremiah 46—49; Matthew 24:15-26

LESSON AIM
To be aware of and avoid the spirit of antichrist.

LEARN BY HEART
"Who is a liar but he that denieth that Jesus is the Christ? He is antichrist, that denieth the Father and the Son" (I John 2:22).

EVERY DAY WITH THE WORD

STUDENT'S NOTEBOOK

This column is for the student who desires additional study of the lesson theme.

Monday	Denying yourself	Matthew 16:21-28
Tuesday	Denying Christ	Acts 3:12-26
Wednesday	Denying the faith	I Timothy 5:1-12
Thursday	Denying the power	II Timothy 3:1-9
Friday	Denying ungodliness	Titus 2
Saturday	Denying the blood	II Peter 2
Sunday	Denying the Lord God	Jude 3-16

LESSON PREPARATION

What is the tremendous attraction in the Middle East that world powers continue to grapple for possession of a relatively small strip of land called Palestine? For one thing, it is a land-bridge between the continents of Africa, Asia, and Europe. Whoever holds this territory controls the destiny of billions of people. Europe gets two-thirds of its oil from the Middle East. The United States would be crippled without access to these oil reserves which are yielding millions of barrels each day. The Dead Sea is worth more than the total wealth of the United States.

These natural resources make the Middle East the coveted prize of world leaders. If Russia could get uncontested control of this geographical treasure chest, she would have no serious contender for world power.

THE ELEVATION OF THE ANTICHRIST (Daniel 11:36-39)

Of all the wicked end-time personalities, which one should be called "the antichrist"? Nothing is more confusing than trying to harmonize all that has been written on this subject. Almost no two books on prophetic themes agree about who the antichrist is specifically. Many are satisfied to pass lightly over the various characters who figure in the tribulation and call all of them "antichrist." Other writers are more careful in delineating precisely which of the leaders is really the antichrist.

John the Apostle is the only Biblical writer who employs the term "antichrist." In John's day many antichrists had already appeared (I John 2:18). John treats the subject of antichrist as if it pertained to a spirit, a system, or a philosophy. But he also speaks of it as a person. The antichrist is foremost a liar and a deceiver (verse 22; II John 7). His special mark of identification is his deceit and fraudulent claims to Messiahship.

The fact that he is known especially for deceit points us immediately to II Thessalonians 2

Wilbur Smith, Walvoord, Pentecost, DeHaan, Newell, Unger, Larkin, Lang, and Ottman put the title on the first beast.

W. E. Blackstone, C. Jennings, Scofield, James Gray, Gaebelein, English, Ironside, Tatham, Tatford, Darby, Williams, Kelly, James Scott, Walter Scott, Tucker, E.W. Rogers put the title "antichrist" on the second beast.

where Paul is describing a deceiver and liar (verses 9,11). In the Thessalonian passage Paul calls the antichrist "the man of sin" because he is the epitome of all wickedness and lawlessness; he calls him "the son of perdition" because he is destined for eternal ruin (verse 3).

Part of the antichrist's deceit involves palming himself off on the Jews as the Son of God—the Messiah. Paul shows that antichrist will occupy the holy of holies in the restored Jewish temple in Jerusalem and demand divine honors and titles (verse 4). His deceit also includes his ability to convince the Jews that he is their Messiah by performing all kinds of wonders and miracles (verse 9).

Who can read Paul's description in II Thessalonians without turning to Revelation 13:11-18 where we have practically the same description of the antichrist in the second beast? Verse 13 speaks of the "great wonders" which he will perform. Verses 14,15 tell of the miracles which he will accomplish to authenticate his claims to be Israel's prophet and king. Antichrist is clearly an imitation christ, a false christ, the false prophet. In every respect he is a substitute christ—even to the extent of posing as a lamb (verse 11).

The fact that the antichrist originates out of the earth (verse 11) suggests that he derives from Israel—the earthly people. He is a Jewish king whom the nation will receive and own as their protector and friend in the tribulation period. As a prophet, he assumes control of religion. Like the prophet Elijah who authenticated his credentials by calling down fire from Heaven, the antichrist will give dramatic evidence of his right to shape all religious policies. As an economist, he will

The psalmist calls the antichrist "the bloody and deceitful man" (Psalm 5:6).

The first beast is never associated with deceit. The second beast is the deceiver and the antichrist as John says (see II John 7 and Revelation 19:20).

John 5:43 speaks of the antichrist who will come posing as Christ. The Jews would not receive the real Messiah when he came, but they will embrace the false christ. It is

control world commerce so that no one can buy or sell without his approval (verses 16,17). The antichrist will place a mark upon his followers (verse 16). It is the visible proof that they are worshipers of the antichrist's ally in Europe (verse 17).

The antichrist is not the sole ruler of the future. He shares equally with the European dictator—the beast out of the sea (Revelation 13:1). The antichrist is not subordinate to the Gentile dictator in the West; "he exerciseth all the power of the first beast before him, and causeth the earth . . . to worship the first beast" (verse 12). The antichrist will sit in the temple and work miracles to demonstrate that he is God. At the same time, he will acknowledge the deity of the first beast and require the Jews to worship the first beast. He will be so ardent in promoting the worship of the European political and military dictator that he will put a statue of the dictator in the temple (Matthew 24:15).

The relationship between the antichrist and the first beast, as defined in Revelation 13, is exactly the same as the relationship described in Daniel 11:36-39. In Daniel's account we learn once more of the antichrist's sovereign power in the expression "the king shall do according to his will" (verse 36). Daniel agrees with Paul's comment about how the antichrist will exalt himself above every god (compare II Thessalonians 2:4 with Daniel 11:36,37). Daniel sees the very same connection between the antichrist and the European dictator that John analyzes in Revelation 13; the antichrist, for all his self-exaltation and claims to deity, nevertheless acknowledges another god (Daniel 11:38,39). The "God of forces" is the first beast of Revelation 13—the Gentile dictator

unthinkable that the Jews would own anyone but a Jew as their Messiah. And they would require credentials of the miraculous. They are expecting Elijah to come to perform miracles. When a greater than Elijah comes, they will receive him.

The New Scofield
Reference Bible
sanctions this view:
"The 'willful king'
disregards the God
of Israel (KJV 'the
God of his fathers');
cares nothing for the
hope of Messiah
('the desire of
[Jewish] women');
and honors the
Roman beast ('the
god of fortresses',
Rev. 13:11-18)."
See page 917.

in Europe who promises military assistance to the antichrist in Palestine. The antichrist secures Western protection by plundering the vast resources of Palestine and sending them to his ally in Europe (Daniel 11:38). Not satisfied with that, the European dictator will insist upon a statue of himself being placed in the Jewish temple. The antichrist will comply and thus share the holy of holies with the image of the first beast. Moreover, the antichrist will dissect Palestine, donating pieces of ground to those Jews who do him favors (verse 39).

Isaiah, Daniel, and John all introduce the antichrist abruptly and without a word of explanation. Isaiah and Daniel simply call him "the king." John calls him the beast out of the earth and later speaks of him as the false prophet. But the antichrist is both a king and a prophet. In this regard he is an imitator of Christ the prophet-king.

THE ENEMIES OF THE ANTICHRIST
(Daniel 11:40-45)

Sometime after the Jewish antichrist has established himself in Palestine as Israel's Messiah, the armies of Egypt will make another attempt to destroy the State of Israel. The humiliation of being defeated again will increase Egyptian hostility against the Jews. Thirst for revenge will drive this Arab nation to further aggression. Without a doubt, Egypt will use equipment supplied to her by Russia.

Joel 2:11 calls the
northern army "his
army"—that is,
God's army. For God
will use this army to
chastise Israel.

But Russia cannot afford to let Egypt gain sole control of the Middle East, and so as soon as Egypt marches northward, Russia will march southward. The Jewish antichrist will face an invasion on both fronts (Daniel 8:24; 11:40). The king of the North (Russia accompanied by Syrian troops) is obviously the victor. The northern armies will sweep through Palestine like a flood of waters. Many other countries are included with the northern aggressor in his drive through the Holy Land (verse 41). Ezekiel 38 tabulates many of the countries which will contribute their armies to the war effort. Isaiah connects the destruction of Lebanon, Syria, Jordan, Israel, and Arabia with the northern invasion. In all likelihood Russia will add the armies of the conquered peoples to her growing military strength as she enters the Middle East.

The first reference to the king of the North associates the army with a flood of waters (Isaiah 8:7,8; see also Isaiah 17:13; 28:2, 15-18; 30:28; Jeremiah 47:2; Daniel 9:26; 11:22; Hosea 5:10; Amos 5:24; Revelation 12:15).

We can only conjecture that Egypt will eventually have a falling out with Russia, who has been supplying her with arms and technicians. It may be that Egypt invades Israel without the sanction of Russia, and so the armies of the North intervene and take advantage of the situation to bring Egypt under Soviet mastery.

The Russian hordes will not stop until they have penetrated to North Africa (Daniel 11:42). Isaiah predicted this long before Daniel wrote. He said that Egypt would capitulate to a king of fierce countenance (Isaiah 19:4; compare Daniel 8:23). In chapter 20 Isaiah also forecast the destruction of Ethiopia by the Assyrian (the king of the North). Ezekiel concurs in his prediction that Persia, Ethiopia, and Libya will be involved in the Russian invasion (Ezekiel 38:5). Now Daniel tells us plainly that the king of the North will conquer Egypt, Libya and Ethiopia (Daniel 11:43).

Isaiah 19 and 20 indicate that Egypt and Ethiopia will fall to the king of the North. Habakkuk 3:6-12 says the same thing.

Read Jeremiah 46:7-10 in this connection. Study Ezekiel 30:3-9. Ethiopia will suffer from an invasion by sea (verse 9).

After the Russians have subdued North Africa and have set up a military headquarters in Egypt, they will receive some disquieting reports from the

Northeast (verse 44). No one knows for certain what causes the concern, but possibly Russia will hear that the European beast-dictator has brought the allied armies to Israel for the purpose of meeting military obligations and in an attempt to cut the Russian armies off from their home base in the Soviet Union. Some expositors, however, think that a report of an Oriental invasion startles the Russians. At any rate, Russia will make a frantic effort to retreat through Palestine to the North.

En route Prince Rosh will decide to annihilate Israel. He wants to make Israel pay for the necessity of his retreat. In this he resembles his ancient predecessor, Antiochus Epiphanes, who was thwarted in Egypt and took his wrath out on the Jews. The Russian armies will have God to reckon with. He will not permit the utter annihilation of the Jews even though He brought the northern armies against them to chastise them for placing their hopes in the Jewish antichrist and his western confederate and for permitting the introduction of idolatry to the land again.

Here is another indication that Antiochus Epiphanes is meant to illustrate the king of the North and not the Jewish antichrist.

Determined now to liquidate Israel, the northern armies will set their sights on Jerusalem. They will get no farther than the mountains south of the city. There God will literally bury the armies of Gog and Magog. A terrific earthquake will cause the ground to swallow up the infantry. Ezekiel graphically describes the scene. Daniel only comments: "yet he shall come to his end, and none shall help him" (verse 45). This harmonizes with what Daniel says earlier about the end of the king of the North: "he shall be broken without hand" (Daniel 8:25). Joel supplements what Ezekiel and Daniel narrate by explaining what happens to any who escape the earthquake.

Both Isaiah and Ezekiel speak about the wicked thought which the king of the North entertains to destroy the Jews. Compare Isaiah 10:7 with Ezekiel 38:10.

They will be driven down into the desert regions south of Israel and perish in the sands (Joel 2:20). During the period of the millennium tourists will come across the parched bones of the army and remember that God wrought a great deliverance in the land (Ezekiel 39:15).

FOOD FOR THOUGHT

"War! that mad game the world so loves to play."

—Jonathan Swift

NOW TEST YOUR KNOWLEDGE

For each of the following, tell which end-time figure is in view:

1. Man of sin
2. False Christ
3. Roman prince
4. Assyrian
5. Successor to Antiochus Epiphanes
6. God of forces
7. Little horn of Daniel 8
8. Antichrist
9. Son of perdition
10. Political ruler
11. "His army"
12. Bloody and deceitful man
13. Ecclesiastical ruler
14. Little horn of Daniel 7
15. *The* king
16. Gog and Magog
17. False prophet
18. Desolator
19. Marine beast
20. Prince Rosh

a. The first beast
b. The second beast
c. The king of the north

When God Writes "Finished"

13

LESSON SCRIPTURE
Daniel 12

RELATED SCRIPTURE
Hosea 13:14; Amos 8:12; II Corinthians 5;
I Thessalonians 4:13-18; Hebrews 11:35

LESSON AIM
To wait patiently, yet eagerly, for the
Lord's return.

LEARN BY HEART
"And they that be wise shall shine as
the brightness of the firmament; and they
that turn many to righteousness as the
stars for ever and ever" (Daniel 12:3).

EVERY DAY WITH THE WORD

STUDENT'S NOTEBOOK

This column is for the student who desires additional study of the lesson theme.

Monday	Resurrection of a widow's son	I Kings 17:17-24
Tuesday	Resurrection of Jairus' daughter	Matthew 9:18-26
Wednesday	Resurrection of Lazarus	John 11:21-44
Thursday	Resurrection of Christ	John 20:1-18
Friday	Resurrection of Dorcas	Acts 9:36-43
Saturday	Resurrection of the saints	I Corinthians 15:35-50
Sunday	Resurrection of two witnesses	Revelation 11:3-14

LESSON PREPARATION

In 1938 Orson Welles broadcast a drama depicting an invasion of earth by spacemen from Mars. This program was so realistic that thousands of Americans thought the end of the world had come. Some lost their sanity; others committed suicide. Until the public realized it was only a fictitious melodrama, pandemonium broke loose.

Men have talked of doomsday and the end of the world for generations, but any Bible believer knows that God has great plans for the world which forbid the end of the world until Christ has reigned on earth for a thousand years.

Daniel talks often about the end of the age, but he does not mean an interplanetary invasion, a global collision, or a geological catastrophe on a universal scale. Rather, he refers to the termination of the times of the Gentiles, the end of Russian aggression, the ruination of the European beast and his false prophet in Jerusalem, the end of wars and bloodshed, the end of Israel's dispersion, and the end of all Christ rejectors and God-denying anarchists.

Doomsday will come at the end of the millennial reign of Christ when the earth and all that is in it will be burned up to prepare for an entirely different order in the new heavens and the new earth (II Peter 3:10-13; Revelation 21:1).

It is true that civilization as we know it will be destroyed during the tribulation.

THE DISTINCTION OF THE TIME
(Daniel 12:1-9)

Michael's prominence (Daniel 12:1) should be associated with several factors: (1) He is the guardian of the nation Israel—their protector and preserver. He is responsible for the continuation of this ancient people who are the only nation to survive from antiquity. (2) He is somehow involved in resurrection. Whenever a resurrection occurs, Michael is on hand to contribute (see Daniel 12:1,2; I Thessalonians 4:16; Jude 9). (3) He is the initiator of a great war in Heaven between his angels and the devil with his demon hosts. Revelation 12 puts this conflict at the midway point in the tribulation (verses 7-12). Jesus alludes to the same event in Matthew 24:29. The

This is a great miracle and one of the proofs that the Bible is true and that God has a great destiny in store for Israel as a nation.

At a later time Satan will be cast down even farther—into the abyss (Revelation 20:1-3).

casting down of Satan to earth and the confinement of his activities here will commence the second half of the tribulation—called by Jesus "great tribulation" (Matthew 24:21; see also Revelation 7:14). Daniel 12:1 speaks of it as the worst calamity that ever has befallen or ever will befall Israel in her long and stormy history.

Michael will assert himself in Israel's defense in that unprecedented hour of trial that will come upon the earth. There is a vast difference between general tribulation and the great tribulation in which God's fearful wrath will be visited upon earth dwellers. General trouble has its source in the machinations of the devil against God's people; the great tribulation has its ultimate source in the wrath of God and is directed without abatement upon godless society. Despite the terrible severity of the tribulation judgments, many of Daniel's people (the Jews) will be delivered (verse 1). They will survive the disasters and be alive at the time of the inauguration of the kingdom age. Those who see it through to the end of the desolation are declared to be "every one that shall be found written in the book" (verse 1). We are assured from this expression and from countless other passages in the prophets that only regenerate Jews will be left alive on the earth by the beginning of the millennium. All of earth's population will greatly diminish and the total number of Jews will be reduced by one third.

See Isaiah 4:3,4; 11:11; 33:14; Ezekiel 20:38; Matthew 13:41,42; 24:39-41. Those who are taken away (Matthew 24) are the wicked who are removed by divine judgment.

Verse 2 contains the first hint in the Bible that the notion of a general, all-inclusive resurrection of both the righteous and the wicked at the same event is false. "Many" will be raised, not all. Many will be raised out from among others who will not be raised at that time. Those who do arise

Isaiah 25:6-9; 26:17-21 refers to the resurrection of the righteous. In the Old Testament only Daniel speaks of the resurrection of the wicked.

107

from the dead at the end of the tribulation will be counted among those who participate in the first resurrection. Daniel calls it a resurrection "to everlasting life" (verse 2). Jesus mentions it in nearly the same terms (John 5:29). Those bodies which are not raised at this time but remain in their graves until the end of the kingdom age will be raised to appear at the great white throne judgment for shame and everlasting contempt, or as Jesus puts it, "unto the resurrection of damnation." Neither Daniel nor Jesus mentions the one-thousand-year interval which will separate these two resurrections. But Paul leaves room for it in I Corinthians 15:23-25; John adds important details in Revelation 20:4-6.

The wicked dead will be raised but they will not have glorified bodies. Even after they are raised they are called "dead" (Revelation 20:12).

Daniel 12:3 alludes to a special group of saved Jews called the "wise." The fulfillment of the promises to Abraham requires the existence of a remnant of elect Jews who will be saved during the tribulation period and become the children of the kingdom. In addition, there is to be distinguished a remnant within the remnant—a special group of 144,000 Jewish instructors, preachers, and teachers. They will be saved and sealed by the Spirit of God immediately after the church saints have been resurrected and raptured. They will be commissioned to take the gospel of redeeming grace—with special emphasis upon the imminence of the coming kingdom—to the world. Their witness during the first half of the tribulation will result in the salvation of countless Jews and Gentiles. They will "turn many to righteousness," and during the millennial age they will enjoy a special prominence, shining "as the stars for ever and ever."

More particularly it is called the gospel of the kingdom (Matthew 24:14; Mark 1:14,15).

Some strange teachings have been based on

Daniel 12:4. Commonly it is taught that we have here a prediction of the jet age and the phenomenal acceleration of learning. Interpreting this verse in its context would correct the popular notion. The angel told Daniel that the book—the book of Daniel—will be a closed volume for unbelieving Jews from that time until the time of the end. The Jews read Daniel and the other prophets without understanding. Today the nation suffers from spiritual blindness—a condition which will not be altered until the event of the rapture of the church. In the time of the end after the translation of church saints, judicial blindness will be lifted; Jews will search thoroughly ("run to and fro") the book of Daniel. The Spirit of God will illumine them, and they will at last increasingly understand the significance of these prophecies. Running to and fro refers to the action of the eyes in perusing a book; it has nothing to do with our travel-conscious age.

Implicit in verse 4 is an explanation of how people will become regenerate in the tribulation period. They will be saved in exactly the same manner in which believers of the church age are saved. God the Holy Spirit is the divine agent; preachers of the grace of God are the human medium; the incorrputible seed of the Word of God is the instrumental means. No one in any dispensation ever got saved in any other way except by the grace of God through faith in the promises.

Isaiah 6:9,10;
Matthew 13:13-15.

II Chronicles 16:9

No dispensational theologian who is careful would ever suggest that God saves men in different ways in different dispensations. The various dispensations are not different methods of salvation.

THE DURATION OF THE TIME
(Daniel 12:10-13)

At best we can only conjecture what may be the

significance of the dates recorded in Daniel 12. Verse 7 puts the terminal point at 1260 days after the erection of the idol in the temple at Jerusalem. This length of time is coincident with the reign of the European dictator-beast (Daniel 7:25; Revelation 13:5), the Gentile control over Jerusalem (Revelation 11:2), the ministry of the two witnesses (verse 3), and the hiding of Israel in the wilderness, possibly at Petra (Revelation 12:14). We can safely assume, then, that at the end of 1260 days the empire of the beast will collapse and with it the beast himself and his Jewish ally.

Daniel 12:11 adds an extra month to the 1260 days. M. R. DeHaan felt it represents a period of grace before Christ destroys the ungodly. Others think it refers to the time required for cleaning up the worst of the debris of war (although apparently this will necessitate much more time—see Ezekiel 39:9,12). One guess is as good as another. If the kingdom of the beast is destroyed by an invasion from the Far East, perhaps the thirty days represent the period of conquest by the Oriental armies and the marshalling of Western troops to confront them at Armageddon. Conceivably, Christ will personally return at the end of these 1290 days to slay the armies of the Oriental host.

Then we are faced with a third date of 1335 days or 45 days beyond the 1290 days. Some expositors have suggested that this will mark the first celebration of the feast of tabernacles which will take place 45 days after the millennial age commences. We can be certain that the 75 days beyond the initial 1260 are essential as a period of preparation for full kingdom blessings. They must indicate some kind of transition period between the tribulation and the millennium. A transition

Not until the armies of the North have been destroyed will the beast gain uncontested dominion over the world of prophecy. For this reason he appears prominently in Revelation 13 and afterward, not before except a mere mention.

It seems that the multitude carrying palms in Revelation 7:9-17 are preparing to celebrate the feast of tabernacles in the millennial age

period separates the Mosaic dispensation from the church dispensation, and we can expect some similar interval between the judgments of the time of trouble and the times of refreshing from the presence of the Lord (Acts 3:19).

Although the tribulation period will fulfill many purposes in the program of God, one of the chief purposes is the salvation and sanctification of a people to whom God can fulfill the covenant promises to Abraham, Moses and David. What will God use to take away the dross and purify the people who are to become the residents of the millennial earth? God will use the fires of the tribulation. The prophets are filled with references to this refining process. During the tribulation many will be cleansed. God will regenerate them and work His own righteousness in them (Daniel 12:10). Trouble has a way of bringing God's elect people to rely wholly upon the Lord.

The tribulation judgments will have no cleansing effect, however, on the apostate Jews. The same sun that melts wax hardens clay. The wicked will not repent amid the outpouring of divine wrath; they will increase in their wickedness (Revelation 6:16,17; 9:20,21; 16:10,11,21).

A special benediction is pronounced upon those saved Jews who patiently wait for the Messiah to come to deliver them from the distresses of the hour of trial (Daniel 12:12). Those who survive until the 1335 days will see the King coming in His glory to the Mount of Olives. They will enter into the millennial age with all of its prosperity, peace, righteousness, and joy. They will be present at the wedding feast celebrated on earth at the beginning of the millennium. Christ and His bride have been joined at the wedding ceremony in

The tribulation is also designed to bring an end to Gentile dominion.

Romans 11:26

Zechariah 12:10

Matthew 25:10

Heaven, and now the ladies in waiting (Israel), the friend of the bridegroom (John the Baptist), and the servants (saved Gentiles) will all participate in the joy of the festive occasion. The waiting regenerate Jews will be blessed because the ancient promises of a restoration of the kingdom to David will be fulfilled to them, and they will be delegated positions of jurisdiction in the kingdom government as a reward for their faithfulness to Christ during the terrors of the beasts' joint reign.

Romans 14:17

Revelation 19:7

FOOD FOR THOUGHT

"Other men see only a hopeless end, but the Christian rejoices in an endless hope."
—Gilbert M. Beenken

NOW TEST YOUR KNOWLEDGE

Answer true or false:
1. The time of the end refers to doomsday.
2. Gabriel is Israel's special defender.
3. Satan and his angels are cast down to earth during the first half of the tribulation.
4. Even the church saints will experience the great tribulation.
5. Daniel 12:2 teaches a general resurrection.
6. The 144,000 Jews from the twelve tribes of Israel will be saved by the grace of God and will be sealed by the Holy Spirit.
7. Daniel anticipated the space age.
8. Tribulation saints will be saved spiritually by enduring unto the end.
9. The significance of the different numbers of days in Daniel 12 is plainly disclosed.
10. The children of the kingdom are the residents of the earthly millennium.